Edited by
SONIA MA

My Gutsy Story® Anthology

②

Inspirational Short Stories
About Taking Chances
and Changing Your Life

GUTSY
PUBLICATIONS

My Gutsy Story® Anthology: Inspirational Short Stories About Taking Chances and Changing Your Life

For information about this title or to order other books and/or electronic media, contact the publisher:

Gutsy Publications
23785 El Toro Road, #131, Lake Forest, CA 92630
www.GutsyPublications.com
Info@GutsyPublications.com

ISBN: 978-0-98540394-2

Printed in the United States of America

Cover and Interior design: 1106 Design

Publisher's Cataloging-in-Publication
(Provided by Quality Books, Inc.)

   My gutsy story anthology : inspirational short stories
      about taking chances and changing your life / edited by
      Sonia Marsh.
         pages cm.
         ISBN 978-0-9854039-4-2
         ISBN 978-0-9854039-5-9

         1. Courage—Anecdotes. 2. Self-realization—
   Anecdotes. 3. Conduct of life—Anecdotes. 4. Love—
   Anecdotes. 5. Biography—Anecdotes.   I. Marsh, Sonia.
   II. Title: Inspirational short stories about taking
   chances and changing your life.

   BJ1533.C8M932 2014   179'.6
                                QBI14-1565

Dedication

To those who are already living a *gutsy* life, and to those who need a nudge to start their own. Everyone has a "My Gutsy Story®"; some of us just need a little help to uncover ours.

My wish is to create a global community where we can feel safe to share our own "My Gutsy Story®" and help one another take risks in life. — Sonia Marsh

Contents

Peter Jones

DOING EVERYTHING, BEING HAPPY

ON MY THIRTY-SECOND BIRTHDAY, as I sat at my mother's dining room table in front of a large cake, thirty-two candles threatening to ignite my beard should I lean too far forward, I realised that the only ambition I had left in life — the only dream I hadn't given up on — was to be married.

Or at least in some sort of steady, loving relationship.

A long-term partnership with someone whose ying was a close match to my less-than-melodic yang.

But even this — this last, naive expectation of life — was looking increasingly unlikely. Every candle on that cake was some sort of burning epitaph to just how utterly rubbish I was when it came to affairs of the heart.

There had been relationships in the past — of course there had — but I'd kind of fallen into them by accident. And after the ladies in question had tried, and failed, to mould me into the kind of man they wanted, those relationships had withered and died. There hadn't been an 'accidental relationship' for a while. Colleagues no longer described me as an eligible bachelor. Some had started to question my sexuality.

So as my family launched into a rendition of "Happy Birthday", I decided there and then that the prospect of being single for the rest of my days was unacceptable.

Something had to be done.

Around that time there was a TV show called *Would Like to Meet*, where a team of experts would take some hapless individual and turn him or her into a heartthrob or a man-magnet. It very quickly became my favourite TV show. I'd watch it avidly from one week to the next, hoping to pick up some tips. And the conclusion I came to was that I, too, could do with a similar makeover — albeit without the entire viewing nation of the United Kingdom looking on.

So over the next few weeks I tracked down image consultants, and I contacted one. Back then, image consultants mainly worked for corporations, restyling senior corporate executives who might otherwise look less than sharp in the boardroom. But I had surprisingly little problem persuading my consultant of choice to broaden the scope of her client base to include one sad and lonely thirty-something guy. She took one look at me, threw away every item of clothing I'd acquired in the previous decade, and in an afternoon gave me some much needed va-va-voom in the wardrobe department.

And once I'd been completely restyled, I looked around for a flirt coach.

These days, you can barely move for self-styled relationship experts and flirt coaches, but back in 2003 I could find just one. And she ran courses.

I took several hundred pounds from my savings, and booked myself on a 'flirting weekend'. Nervously, I took my place in the front row and, when instructed, turned and introduced myself to the stunning blonde sitting next to me.

"I'm Peter," I said.

"I'm Kate," said the blonde.

Then she smiled.

And I was smitten.

The course wasn't that much of a success, in that it didn't teach me how to flirt. Not that it mattered. My strategy had worked, somewhat differently but infinitely better than I'd hoped. On the Monday evening, Kate and I had our first date. By the Tuesday I'd officially found myself a girlfriend. A few months later I found myself on one knee. And a year to the day after we first met, I found myself married.

And when she died in my arms just two years later, I was heartbroken.

People rarely ask me how Kate died. It's not the sort of question they feel comfortable asking. Most assume she must have had cancer — that we'd have had some warning. We didn't.

I've learnt since that sudden deaths like Kate's (a subarachnoid haemorrhage) are surprisingly common. Kate had a weak part in her brain, probably since birth. It could have happened at any moment. It was almost inevitable.

I learnt, too, that after the shock comes the guilt. Every cross word, every nasty thought, every lie — they all come back to haunt you. And among the demons that were queuing up to torment me was the realisation that I still wasn't happy, and maybe I never had been. There had been happy moments, of course. Quite a lot of moments. Most of them in the previous three years, and most of them down to Kate; but they were moments nonetheless. And I wanted to be happy all the time. Not just occasionally. Not just for a moment.

Something had to be done.

I decided to tackle the problem the only way I knew how: by making lists and coming up with a strategy.

"So what," people ask, "is in this … 'happiness strategy'?"

I tell about my 'Now List', my 'Wish List', how I set myself yearly goals, and how I make sure I actually achieve them.

I tell them how I've taken back control of my life, decided how I want it to be, pointed it in that direction, and given it a kick up the backside.

I tell them how I'm having more fun than I've ever had. Smiling more than I ever did. How there's love in my life again. How I think Kate would be proud of me. And that I can finally say, I'm happy.

PETER JONES started professional life as a particularly rubbish graphic designer, followed by a stint as a mediocre petrol pump attendant. After that he got embroiled in the murky world of credit card banking, where he developed 'fix-it-man' superpowers.

Now, Peter spends his days — most of them, anyway — writing. He is the author of three-and-a-half popular self-help books on the subjects of happiness, staying slim, and dating. If you're overweight, lonely, or unhappy — he's your guy.

Find out more about Peter Jones, his books, speaking engagements and workshops, at www.peterjonesauthor.com

Destiny Allison

IN AN INSTANT

I N AN INSTANT, MY WORLD COLLAPSED. It wasn't just the absence of planes in the sky or the way people wandered around blank and numb. By then I'd turned off the news, not wanting my young children to be more frightened than they already were. Like most, I did what I had to do to get through the days. I even bought a flag and hung it on my porch — solidarity with my country, grief for what had been lost. I went to work, interacted with a new boss I couldn't stand, and did my job. Until, that is, I didn't have one.

The Sept. 11, 2001, terrorist attack had destroyed the economy and crushed the annual fundraiser our small nonprofit depended upon. As fast as the planes had hit the buildings, and with the same shock of disbelief and terror, I was unemployed.

I was a single mom, raising my three children alone. There was little in the way of child support, only a pittance in my savings account, and a new mortgage I couldn't afford. Everything in me froze. Where would I find a job? How would I care for my kids? Through long and sleepless nights, I stared at the ceiling, my heart racing. Then as winter crept up frost-covered windows, something in me started to thaw. Could my layoff have been a gift? Was there a message in all of this?

I had been an artist for years, wrestling my clay and wax at night and on weekends when my children were sleeping or occupied. I had placed a few pieces in local galleries and even sold some, but never enough to let me quit my proverbial day job. Making art was the only thing I never gave up on, the only thing that offered my hard life a measure of relief. In those cold days between Thanksgiving and Christmas, while I worried how to keep the heat on, a voice kept whispering, "Now or never, girl. It's now or never."

I made the leap. Instead of job hunting, I started making things, submitting my portfolio to shows, and praying. Instead of reacting to my circumstances, I would change them, take control of my life for the first time, and become the woman I wanted to be.

The first show was hard, but I sold just enough to pay my bills and get to the next one. I learned everything I could about my new business and applied it quickly. The second show was a little better. By summer, I was making more money than my old job had paid me. It was hard. Really, really hard, but I was doing it.

I worked seven days a week, building sculptures as fast as I could. Some of them I didn't like, some were OK, and others had that glimmer of something that made me catch my breath. It didn't matter what I thought about the work. It sold. All of it. What I thought was terrible brought a buyer to tears. The art moved people.

I learned how to talk about my work and share the personal stories that inspired the pieces. I learned how to price, when to spend money and when to save it, and how to be myself. Instead of dressing to impress, I dressed for comfort so I wasn't self-conscious while selling my work. Every six weeks I took to the road for a week or two. I hired nannies — something I will always regret — missed my kids, and worried they would feel I had abandoned them. In some ways, I did. But I had no choice. They needed food, clothes, a roof over their heads, and a decent education. Their teenage years were hard on all of us. Every time I wondered whether I was doing the right thing, I thought that if I gave up my passion, I would teach them to do the same. I couldn't live with that, so I chose to model what it takes to make it — and spent as much time with them as I could.

Fast forward twelve years. My children are grown, and I am proud of them. They are wonderful, self-sufficient, and kind. I met the love of my life and married him. I am internationally collected, exhibited by top galleries, and living the dream come true.

Then, unexpectedly and in the weirdest way, I threw my back out permanently. My studio days are numbered, my income is dropping, and all of a sudden I'm writing. I released *Shaping Destiny* last year. It is the story of how I found my voice as an artist. Having just released my second book, *Pipe Dreams*, I am reminded of that first journey. Like then, I'm facing a road that is long and hard, but I trust it will be infinitely rewarding.

I can do this. I can face my fears and conquer my misgivings. That little voice is whispering again. "Now or never, girl," it says. The difference this time is that I know who I am, what I can do, and have a family that understands and supports my process. Because I believe in myself, they do, too.

DESTINY ALLISON: Destiny Allison is an award-winning sculptor, businesswoman, and community builder, but writing was her first love. Last year, she published *Shaping Destiny: A Quest for Meaning in Art and Life*. The nonfiction work was recently awarded first place for nonfiction/memoir in the 2013 Lucky Cinda Global Book Contest.

Pipe Dreams is her fiction debut, and other fictional works are soon to follow. Allison believes that our lives are our greatest works of art and that we have to be who and what we are, not who and what we're supposed to be. This theme is reflected in her written works, sculptures, and business endeavors. Allison lives in Santa Fe, New Mexico, with her husband and dogs, alternately missing and celebrating her three grown sons. Website: www.DestinyAllison.com

Penelope James

WHAT DO YOU DO WHEN THE GOOD TIMES END?

MY ADVERTISING CAREER STARTED in London and ended in Mexico City in 1990 when my boss persuaded me to take early retirement. I heard "corporate takeover casualties," but he was so smooth that for several minutes I didn't understand that he meant "you're fired."

After I agreed to resign in exchange for a hefty sum, he asked, "What will you do next?"

"I'll get rid of my high heels, give away my business suits, let my hair grow down to my waist — and strangle you with my pantyhose. Then, I'll open a restaurant." I'd been toying with this idea for a while. Just needed the money to get it going. With my severance package, marketing savvy, and cooking expertise, I knew it would be a success. Provide me with an income for life. At forty-six, I had high expectations.

Handling millions of dollars of other people's money was easy compared to handling my own. There'd always been someone to go to the bank for me and help with my accounts and investments. Now I had to do them myself. Maybe I had a flutter of unease when I invested all of my money in this venture, took out loans and used credit cards up to the hilt, but I never expected I'd lose it all. My heart was not in this business; it was more like a romance on the rebound after the end of a long-time relationship.

The restaurant folded after a year, leaving me broke, rudderless, with no idea of where I was heading — except, it seemed, downward.

One morning a sudden urge woke me before dawn, and I wrote the first chapter of a novel that would become my companion for nine years. I completed a full draft in four-and-a-half months, right before my fiftieth birthday. Set in both contemporary and 18th century Mexico, my book had two protagonists and two plots. Overambitious, perhaps, but it kept me going through loss of business, money, status, and my home of 16 years. Gave me a goal. By my mid-fifties I'd be a published author and over this economic hump.

Catering provided an income, though not enough to keep up my former lifestyle. I sold half my belongings and moved to an apartment with a view of the Valley of Mexico. This inspired me to enter a world of mysticism, witches, brews, spells, and past-life experiences that all became fodder for the book. I taught business English and catered events until one afternoon an earthquake rocked my building and sixteen trays of hors d'oeuvres slid off tables and smashed on the floor. I lost my best client, my income plunged, and I fell behind with the rent. My landlord agreed to take my living room furniture and most valuable painting in lieu of what I owed him.

I downscaled to a bungalow — former servants' quarters — and plodded through a second draft. I wrote my frustrations, disappointments, fears into the pages, and the book became Gothic dark. An aching hip slowed me down.

A friend offered me a three-month house-sitting job in Santa Fe, New Mexico, with the bait that I'd have time to write. I ended up stranded, sleeping at her home between house-sitting gigs until she turned unfriendly. Tried pet-sitting. A client asked would I sleep with his basset hound, meaning on the bed with me. A large, solid, tank-like dog that dribbled? My refusal didn't bode well for my career as a pet-sitter.

My computer conked out, so I wrote the old-fashioned way, by hand. My protagonists faced significant obstacles, as did I. A doctor diagnosed degeneration of my hip. I needed an operation. When? A year at most, depending on my tolerance to pain.

My hip deteriorated; I couldn't walk without a cane. I exchanged Santa Fe for life as an invalid in my son's apartment in Tijuana, a city on the Mexican/U.S. border. A doctor promised treatment to help regenerate cartilage. For eighteen months I believed I was making progress, even as the biting pain in my thigh grew worse. I wrote another two drafts of my book, a masterpiece of drama, supernatural happenings, and sex. Since I wasn't getting any, it helped to write about it.

My mother died and left a life insurance that covered a hip replacement. Within weeks of the operation I was ambulant again, and I set out on a job search in San Diego. With no business contacts there, no car, no phone, and almost no money, it meant, at fifty-six, trudging the streets looking for work instead of inhabiting an executive suite.

First I interviewed in ad agencies, where I came face-to-face with young MBAs bristling with Internet know-how and new marketing techniques. Next, want ads. Not computer savvy. Not qualified. Overqualified. A *"We're Hiring"* banner offered a stopgap measure — a job as a phone researcher. $8 an hour. What a comedown, but the 1 to 9 p.m. shift was convenient for commuting across the border.

I became Susan — my first name — J. Whatever happened to Penelope who worked in solitary splendor in an elegant office? Now one of the hundred interviewers in the phone room, I sat in a cubicle wherever supervisors placed me. Another low-wage worker.

For four months I commuted four-and-a-half hours until I saved enough to move to the U.S. My new home was a hotel room. I wrote an eighth draft of my book. Gave my protagonists some happiness. They deserved it after all they had gone through.

Easy work, easy life. A two-year trap in a nothing job. An offer to work as a Hispanic research report writer put me back on track. In two weeks I made the same as in three months in the phone room. A new career beckoned. I could afford an apartment with a view of San Diego Bay. I shelved my book and started writing a riches-to-rags memoir.

Time to move on to the next stage in my life.

PENELOPE JAMES: Anglo-Mexican-American. Born in England, moved to Mexico City at 10. Worked in advertising agencies in New York, London, and Mexico City, and in Hispanic Research in the U.S. Author of *Don't Hang Up! Dialing My Way to a New Start* to be published this autumn. Co-writer of *Barriers to Love,* a memoir by Marina Peralta. Currently lives in San Diego, California.

Former Spanish-English translator, copywriter, report writer, columnist "Insights into Mexico" for *The Baja News.* Has published nonfiction short stories. A judge for the San Diego Book Awards since 2010. Website: www.donthangupbook.com

Jennifer Richardson

THE CASE OF THE MISSING
BIOLOGICAL CLOCK

IN 2005, I QUIT MY JOB in Los Angeles and moved to London with my British husband. You might think moving to a new country is the heart of my gutsy story, but it's really just a backdrop. My real gutsy story is about how, while living in England, I finally made the decision not to have kids.

This decision may not seem gutsy to everyone. Accusations of selfishness abound for the childless by choice. And as if societal pressures weren't enough, my own self-judgment was also a factor. Did my lack of desire to be a mother make me less of a woman? What was wrong with me? And where the hell was my biological clock — and why had it failed to start ticking?

In fairness, there had been indications earlier in my life that I wasn't destined for motherhood. Take, for example, how as a teenager I used to stand in front of the microwave when it was on and proclaim that I was irradiating my uterus to prevent impregnation. (In retrospect, I'm pretty sure I did that because I enjoyed shocking my mother.) Then later, as my friends started to have babies, I was not blind to my uncanny ability to make infants cry instantly upon contact.

But still, some part of me held out for the possibility that I would change my mind. This was what was supposed to happen, right? After all, I had grown up in the eighties when well-meaning feminists were still pushing the belief that women could and should do it all: husband, kids, and a glass-ceiling-breaking career where you got to wear jewel-colored power suits with linebacker-worthy shoulder pads. Convinced I, too, could and should want to do it all, in my late twenties I even went as far as to threaten to break off my engagement to my anti-children fiancé if he wasn't willing to leave open the possibility that one day we might have kids. He caved, and I was a married woman at twenty-nine.

Then, in what seemed like the blink of an eye, thirty-five arrived, and there was still no sign of my biological clock. This state of affairs made me uneasy. I knew beyond that age I was entering into high-risk territory for a pregnancy. In addition, my parents were highly vocal about their desperation for grandchildren and my husband — eager to know once and for all if his life was going to involve children or not — was becoming as vocal as my parents in expressing his desire for me to make a decision already. This is where my story takes a not-so-gutsy turn: I caved to the pressure and, that Christmas, my husband and I announced to my parents that we were going to "try" for a baby in the next year.

But even this game of chicken I had played with myself and my poor, unsuspecting family was not enough to kick-start my biological clock. This became clear as the next year wore on and, each month, I somehow ended up at the pharmacy to pick up a refill of birth control pills. Despite the fact that I was still uneasy, I was finally starting to admit to myself that I didn't really want to have kids.

Later that year I ended up in a neurologist's office with what turned out to be symptoms of multiple sclerosis. It was a development that left my husband and parents as shocked as I was, and temporarily took the focus off the fact that I still hadn't tried to get pregnant. As I grappled with the nature of that disease, which is unsettlingly mysterious in its cause, treatment, and prognosis, I tried desperately to get my neurologist to articulate something I could do that would lessen my chances of developing the full-blown ailment. After evading my previous attempts to pin him down, he finally caved at a follow-up appointment, half-heartedly mentioning a study that had shown some evidence pregnancy would reduce my risk. I couldn't have been more shocked if he had said voodoo might help.

And that's the moment when I realized I didn't want to have kids. This was as good a reason as I was ever going to get to have a child, and yet my gut instantly said no. (Not to mention that as a strategy for lessening my chances of developing a chronic disease, pregnancy seemed at best risky and at worst unethical.) It's been four years since that day, and, although I have since been diagnosed with MS — which in my case just means I have had a second bout of temporary and relatively benign symptoms — I can honestly say I have no regrets about my decision, other than the fact that I didn't have the confidence to make it sooner.

JENNIFER RICHARDSON is the author of *Americashire: A Field Guide to a Marriage*, the 2013 Indie Reader Discovery Award winner for travel writing. The memoir chronicles her decision to give up city life for the bucolic pleasures of the British countryside whilst debating the merits of motherhood. *Americashire* is out now from She Writes Press, and you can find Jennifer online at: www.americashire.com

Liz Burgess

TIME TO LET GO

I HAD A FIVE-HOUR DRIVE TO let reality sink in. I left behind some great friends and a job that I loved, a house full of memories and the feel of warm hugs from my kids at a moment's notice. After 17 years, I was moving from St. Louis, Missouri, to join my husband who had started a job in Chicago, Illinois. My four adult children were excited to be on their own. My son agreed to stay in the house and keep an eye on everything until we were sure that the windy city would become our new home. All I had with me were the dog and my clothes. Oh, and I was six months into a 12-Step program for food addiction. What the heck was I thinking? I was thinking that I didn't bring enough tissues!

Ten years earlier, my husband took a job in Boston. He commuted for about six months. I finally gathered the courage to tell him that I didn't want to move to the East Coast. I told him, "I'm not pulling the kids out of school and away from their friends." I also didn't want to leave my friends, especially since I had already done that once before. The kids don't remember the move from California to Missouri. However,

I remember it and how desperately I missed my friends and family. It took me two years to finally feel "at home" in that new house. Now, I was going to be facing that feeling of not being "at home" all over again.

Our new home is a one-bedroom apartment (a far cry from our four-bedroom house with a huge backyard) that sits on a busy street, with all of the accompanying sounds of bustling city traffic. I had forgotten about our early days of apartment living, and the lack of privacy one has with common-wall neighbors. If I can hear them cough or sneeze, they surely can hear my conversations with the dog, or for that matter, with myself! It's amazing what I've learned about my neighbors without any exchange of conversation!

I chose to make this move because I felt guilty for asking my husband to give up the Boston job. The timing seemed good for everyone involved. The kids were almost all out (or wanting to be) on their own, I was going to have three months of down time (my previous job was at a school and it was summer), and it seemed like a good time to start the "empty nest" phase of my life. By making the move, I would not be able to fall back into old habits of enabling my children or myself. It was time for me to grow up. I needed this fresh start, even if I didn't want it!

Finding a job was difficult for me. Filing for unemployment was out of the question as I had never worked in the new state; I couldn't collect from the old state since I no longer lived there. I was fortunate to get hired for holiday help in retail and was ecstatic when they asked me to stay on after the season was finished. I can't say that it's my Dream Job, but it has been a great learning experience for me and has allowed me to have flexibility with my life and new friends.

I've been in the new home for about a year now, and still feel as though it is temporary. I've kept my old driver's license and car registration, and I have yet to begin moving any of my stuff from the old house "just in case." Letting go is not one of my strong points, but I am learning. Working the Steps of my program of recovery has helped me let go of many things I thought I would have with me forever. Every now and then I catch a glimpse of the light ahead and am able to shed one more layer of something unnecessary in my life, including some bad habits, some weight, and some really nasty feelings.

Anyone who is working a program of recovery knows the range of feelings that one can experience. Some days are filled with agony, white-knuckling, and despair. On the other hand, the good days are filled with joy, hope, and a sense of well-being that makes life full of adventure and new possibilities. My program, and the people I've come to know through it, have been my saving grace.

When I start to feel a little sorry for myself, I look for another glimpse of light and remember how far I've come, and how the difficulty of letting go has eased. I thank God for texting and Facebook, as they both give me the feeling of connection. I now rely a little more on the Big Guy in the Sky and try to have more faith and patience in my everyday living. The answers will come when I'm supposed to know them. The dream job will appear when I'm ready for it. The people who mean the most to me will not be far, even if it is a bit of a drive. It's all going to be okay.

LIZ BURGESS: Born and raised in Southern California, Liz can still conjure up the smells of the beach in a heartbeat. While raising four children, she began documenting their antics and, in the process, realized that writing was just as enjoyable as eating chocolate. Liz has been writing all of her life, but only recently began taking herself seriously. Her blog, "No Excuses — Musings of a Procrastinator," began as a self-improvement commitment and has been a terrific platform for improving her writing, networking with other writers, and stepping outside of her comfort zone, all of which have been very rewarding.

Website: www.noexcuses318.blogspot.com

Sharon Leaf

I Sailed the Seven Seas on a World War II Ship ... and Lived to Tell About It

*~ You cannot discover new oceans until you are
willing to lose sight of the shore ~*
—André Gide

I HAD ONCE DREAMED OF TRAVELING the world for God. But then in 1984, there was the divorce. As a single mom of two, I shelved that dream ... until 1988, when I married my Prince Charming in my forty-second year.

After the fall of Soviet Union Communism in 1991, Rob and I were invited to assist in the new Christian schools in Estonia and Russia. My mind raced: *Go to Russia? Are you crazy?* Then a voice within asked, *Are you going to let fear rule you?* Shoulders back, I took a deep breath of faith, blew out every ounce of fear, and in the dead of winter, I was on my first international journey. From Tallinn to Tartu, from Leningrad to Moscow, for two weeks I soaked in new traditions, unfamiliar languages and delicious foods, but best of all, I met warm and caring people along the way.

After returning home, we felt God calling us to attend an international Bible college in Sweden, but I reasoned away the idea. *We can't leave our jobs, our ministry, and our family for a year.* Then one night as I struggled for sleep, a challenging thought came: *Don't you want to live your dream?* Faith swept over my tired body, and in the summer of '91 two expats leased their home, sold their cars, bid farewell to family and friends, and boarded a jet plane for Sweden.

Our year was full of learning, from books to museums, but it was the people who taught us valuable lessons. I'm grateful to my Swedish neighbor who took me shopping at the centrum market and showed me that mayonnaise came in a tube instead of a jar. Later that evening after brushing his teeth, Rob informed me that Swedish toothpaste was yummy … tasted like mayonnaise. Oops.

After graduation, we toured Israel, and then joined a team in St. Petersburg, Russia, to live for a month on the former Youth Communist propaganda train to distribute humanitarian aid throughout Siberia. There we were — twenty-five Russians, twenty-five Swedes, and the two Americans. Via interpreters, English was the main language spoken, but there were moments when I had to flee to our tiny cabin to escape the constant blending of Russian, Swedish, and Swenglish — a humorous combination of Swedish and English — to keep my head from spinning off. And heaven forbid if I left the train without my day's supply of toilet tissue tucked in my pockets! (I learned the value of used newspapers, which most hospitals, orphanages, and homes supplied upon request.)

The Russians' kindness made every inconvenience fade and erased my doubts about traveling in the once-feared country, but I couldn't wait to touch American soil again. There would always be short trips, but to live abroad again? Never. Until …

Two years later, a flyer crossed our path asking for volunteers to work on a World War II ship that was moored in Seattle, Washington.

Its sole purpose would be to rescue Russian Jews from the Black Sea and take them to Israel. Rob was ready to set sail. Not me. I didn't want anything to upset my comfortable lifestyle, and I certainly had no desire to live on an old troop transport the government had stored in mothballs after the war. She had had only 93 running days, so there was no guarantee that her maiden voyage could even make the journey from Seattle to Stockholm, much less sail to the Black Sea and Israel.

But I wondered, *Could this dangerous assignment mean an adventure of a lifetime? Hmm, this must be where faith must kick in — again.* So in spite of my fear of water and the unknown condition of the ship, the expats once again packed up, leased the house, quit jobs, sold cars, and bid farewell to their safe harbor. God had new oceans waiting.

As we sailed the seven seas, it didn't take this lady long to fall in love with another lady, the MS Restoration. However, it was sometimes a stretch to love thy neighbor while living in such close quarters ... a cabin large enough for a bed and four gym-size lockers, and shared dining experiences with a forty-plus crew in a small troop mess that often smelled like diesel oil. I often asked while cleaning stained toilets and hairy showers, *God, what am I doing here?*

Fourteen months on board the Restoration reminded me of life's simple lessons: You don't need a lot of stuff to be happy — four gym lockers will do. Instead of criticizing (why do Swedish cooks serve pancakes and — yuk — pea soup for lunch?), take time to understand their customs. Instead of judging (why does *she* have special privileges?), practice patience and find out. And no matter how small, boring, or unthankful the task, it is a very big, exciting, and thankful event in God's eyes. Today, I remind myself of these lessons as I clean my own toilets and showers.

You're probably wondering why I had to live on a WWII ship to learn these simple lessons. I asked myself that question often, until one night while we were sailing across the Black Sea. As I gazed at the stars, a familiar voice spoke to my heart, *I have chosen you to be a small part of my big plan to help bring my people home to Israel in these last days*. From that moment, I felt honored to have been on this amazing journey.

The Titanic was called the ship of dreams, but the MS Restoration was God's ship of miracles. Donations of food, ship parts, fuel, bedding, and towels for the crew and the Russian Jews — the list goes on — were given by individuals and various companies. But the greatest miracle was our changed hearts. Living on the MS Restoration truly restored everyone's faith in God, in human kindness, in relationships, and in faith for forgotten dreams. And the dreams continue.

I wish you smooth sailing and oceans of blessings toward your forgotten dreams.

SHARON LEAF: Born in South Carolina and raised in Southern California, since turning forty, Sharon Leaf has traveled to over sixteen countries, lived in Sweden, traveled on the Trans-Siberian Railway, and sailed 26,000 miles on the WWII ship, MS Restoration, to transport Russian Jews from Russia to Israel. She received a degree in theology at sixty, proving that it's never too late to fulfill another dream. *Lady and the Sea,* based on a true story, is Sharon's debut novel. She lives in South Carolina with her husband and keeps busy swimming, Zumba-ing, and writing. Website: www.sharonleaf.com

Dixie Diamanti

BREAKING THE SILENCE

IN HORROR, I STARED AT MY 11-year-old daughter as she, with tears running down her rosy cheeks, recounted the times and places my own father had molested her.

I was torn from my place of denial with a vengeance that knew no mercy. A war waged inside of me. The little girl in me who had never faced her own issues and the mother who was always overly protective fought for freedom from reality. The very thing I thought I had so protected her from had happened. I was in shock.

The stark realization began to sink in as I tried to make sense of everything I had been thrust into. I was 35 years old and had never told a soul that I, too, was an incest survivor. I was totally convinced I would go to the grave with the "secret." Now, because of my silence and denial, my own precious little girl, whom I thought I had protected with my life, had fallen victim to the very same thing I had endured. "Dear God, how does one survive so much pain?" I prayed. I honestly thought my heart would break. My whole foundation of belief was shaken to the core.

I had convinced myself that I would never again have to deal with what happened to me as a child between the ages of seven and twelve. I had vivid memories of every incident down to the details, but until that moment, I had felt nothing emotionally. I taught myself as a little girl to separate from my body when I couldn't deal with the trauma. The real me floated on the ceiling playing with the butterflies while watching what was going on below. I would feel sorry for the little girl below, because she looked so sad. I was just glad it wasn't happening to me.

Interestingly enough, I had been in ministry for years, teaching and praying for the needs of other women, when the force of my own past hit me like a ton of bricks. I slowly realized that, just like the women I ministered to, I must begin the journey of walking through the pain of what happened to me to reach the shores of deliverance. I had been in denial for so many years. I had no idea where the journey would take me, and I was scared. But I knew I had to break the silence, and I started with my daughter.

I went to work immediately to give my daughter all the care and love I had so desperately needed as a child, but never got. My mom instincts took the place of my own victimization. I listened, validated, and comforted her with assurance that I totally believed her and would be there continually as she worked through her emotions. I didn't realize it at the time, but in validating her, I was also validating myself, as no one had ever done for me.

Confronting and exposing my father within my family was the hardest thing I ever had to do. But I knew if I didn't, the incest would continue. I felt like a wicked person forcing my mom to look at the truth. It was horrible and heartbreaking for me to watch her pain at my disclosure. But she soon accused me of lying and regressed into denial, which she had always been good at. Our relationship was never the same after that. She could not accept the truth. She did confront my dad, but somehow they excused themselves of any responsibility and continued living as if it never happened.

I eventually had to release any expectations of her and accept the fact I could not change her, nor make things better for her. The moment I released her from any expectations was the beginning of freedom for me. And when I realized I would receive nothing emotionally from either of them, I released myself from the responsibility of protecting anyone ever again from this kind of violation, nor would I keep their secret. I *was* the victim. But that is the day I became a "survivor." And that was the day the generational pattern of incest was stopped in my family.

At that point, I knew my grandchildren would not be victims of the same crime. The darkness had been exposed to the light. The power of the "secret" was gone. I felt empowered and free from the entanglements and emotions of the past.

Today, my daughter and I both are still learning to "live loved" by our real "Father" in Heaven.

DIXIE DIAMANTI is a Certified Life Coach, author, speaker, and teacher. Dixie has reached out to women and men on the Central Coast of California for many years, leading them into freedom. She believes that every child of God has a distinct calling, and through her work, she assists and coaches individuals in finding their unique purpose in life. Dixie loves to encourage and challenge clients to move forward in uncovering and making use of the hidden treasures within themselves through the coaching process of self-discovery. She is a wife, mom, and nana to a large and supportive family. Website:www.reflectionsofgracehome.com

Don Dempsey

BIRTH

"Listen, I need you to understand what we're up against going in," the doctor said again. His almost serene manner was infuriating. He kept gazing at me like he was waiting for me to understand, or explode. "There is a very real possibility the baby won't make it. You will need to be strong for your wife."

My wife was a nineteen-year-old girl in a room down the hall. She was currently hooked up to so many tubes and machines that it was hard to look at her without fainting. She was pale and frightened, and in pain. It was more than six weeks before the baby's due date, and she'd lost nearly twenty pounds instead of gaining weight like a normal, healthy mother-to-be. Her appearance was haunting and surreal.

I felt more helpless and scared than at any other time in my life.

"I understand."

"We expect the baby to weigh somewhere between 2 and 2½ pounds, and we've taken every precaution. I have a specialist here who will take charge of the baby as soon as we deliver. Your wife will probably require some special attention during and after delivery." He leaned forward and peered at me to stress his next point, his eyes widening a bit. "If you can't remain calm and supportive, it would be best if you waited this out with her family."

Afterward, I washed my face with water and caught my reflection in the mirror above the sink. I was looking pretty haggard myself. Little sleep, long hours in the factory where I worked, and the stress of my wife's difficult pregnancy were taking a toll. I noticed my hands trembling. My breathing was irregular. My heart was pumping so loudly I could hear it.

Without planning to I reached over and locked the door, then flicked off the light. I could still see a shadow of myself in the mirror. There was a hum of activity on the other side of the door. I hated myself for feeling so weak. I detested being afraid. My normal response to these emotions was anger. I could get downright hostile when pushed. Such a response would do me no good in my present situation. In fact, such a response *never* did me any good. I just hadn't learned that valuable lesson yet.

I dropped my head and began to talk. My hands gripped the cool porcelain of the sink. My words were quiet, but earnest and sincere. I wasn't religious, but I did believe in God. I had learned a few things about churches and pastors, none of them pleasant. But I found myself praying nonetheless, hoping that God would hear me and take pity on my wife and unborn son. It didn't take long until I was on my knees and begging.

I promised I would be a better father than the man I had never known had been to me. I beseeched God for the chance to break the cycle of pain and despair I'd been born into. My troubled childhood and a stint in the Marine Corps had transformed me into a young man who was hard to get close to. Dropping my pride wasn't easy. I had always counted on myself during tough times. It would be years before life would teach me how important humility truly is.

As I composed myself, I felt the familiar anger rising, but I squelched it. I knew I was at a crossroads. I had come so far, overcome so much.

I'd worked hard to put the past behind me. But I knew if something happened to my wife or son I was going to suffer terribly. I didn't think I'd be able to get past such a tragedy. I wasn't sure I had the capacity to deal with any more pain.

A few grueling hours later I was peering through a glass window at my infant son. My wife was resting comfortably. It hadn't been easy, but she'd done it. I was certain it was going to be many years before I recovered from the harrowing experience we'd just survived. As low as I'd been before the delivery, I now found myself surging with hope and promise. I couldn't stop smiling. I kept touching the glass and leaning toward my son, straining to get a better look. I had never been happier than at that moment.

A man next to me chuckled. "Your first?" I barely glanced at him but nodded. "Yeah, I can tell." He didn't sound nearly as excited as I was. "Which one's yours?"

I pointed. A nurse was still attending my son, taking blood from the sole of one of his feet. He was squirming and giving her hell. "The good-looking one," I told him.

"A boy," he muttered. "Good for you. That's my third girl over there." I glanced in the direction he indicated and smiled just to be polite. "You won't be nearly so excited the second or third time around."

I wasn't listening to him any longer. What did he know? My son was going to change my life. He was going to prove to the world that I was worth something. He was going to be everything I felt I was never given the chance to be. Everyone would see. All that I never had would be his. I'd see to that. No matter how many hours I had to work, there would be no sacrifice I wouldn't make. He was going to want for nothing and have everything.

My life changed drastically that day. Almost every decision I made from that point on was focused on that boy. He became my reason for living. I pushed for the best grades and accepted nothing less. I demanded success from him in every athletic endeavor, and there were many. And

I never forgot my promise to God. I gave him everything I never had, and I never walked away.

The poor kid.

DON DEMPSEY experienced childhood abuse and neglect firsthand, but went on to have a fulfilling family life as an adult and to own his own business. *"If you're lucky, you make it to adulthood in one piece,"* says Don. *"But there's no guarantee the rest of your life is going to be any better. Abused kids are often plagued by fear and insecurity. They battle depression and have trouble with relationships. In the worst cases, abused children perpetuate the cycle."* But Don is living proof that you can overcome a childhood of abuse and neglect. *"You start by letting go of as much of the guilt (yes, abused kids feel guilty) and as many of the bad memories as possible. At the same time, you hold on to the things that helped you survive. For me, it was the belief that you can make life better by working at it and earning it. It helps to have a sense of humor, too."* Website: www.omishdon.wix.com/bettyschild

Janet Givens

LEAVING A LIFE I LOVED: WHEN THE PEACE CORPS BECKONED

*"I'd rather regret the things I've done than
regret the things I haven't done."*
—Lucille Ball

I JOINED THE PEACE CORPS on June 10, 2004. I was fifty-five and my
husband, Woody, was ten years older. The application process took us
two years — as long as our commitment to the Peace Corps would be.

I'd initially ignored my husband's suggestion two years earlier that
I "just check out their website." But after two weeks of seeing him so
excited by the idea, I finally did.

He'd sprung his "I think we should join the Peace Corps" idea in
late May of 2002. At that time we'd not yet been married three years
and — critical piece here — he'd retired the year before. For nearly thirty
years, he'd been a professor of speech science at Temple University in

Philadelphia and had traveled and written widely in his chosen subfield, stuttering. He was looking for a new challenge. I was not.

I already had a life I loved, including a new career. After a lifetime in the nonprofit world raising money and organizing volunteers, I'd completed an extensive three-year training in Gestalt psychotherapy. Five years earlier, I had opened what came to be an inherently rewarding private practice in the living room of my three-story Italianate home on Philadelphia's west side.

I also loved playing host parent with Woody to foreign students living on our third floor. They generally came from parts of Asia and South America, and were enrolled in the University of Pennsylvania's ESL program. The students filled our home with youthful energy, new ways of seeing the world, and a very nice rental income.

It was a life I envisioned having into my eighties. But the Peace Corps had been a dream of mine since I'd watched my college classmates join and go off to parts unknown nearly forty years before. I hadn't applied in 1971 because I was sure the stuttering I'd struggled with since childhood would keep me out.

By 2002, my stuttering had been a non-issue for many years. Besides, Woody felt that if we were ever going to go, this was the time — he wasn't getting any younger, after all. Browsing through the Peace Corps website, reading about the places we could go, people we could meet, work that was waiting for us, I was smitten. Within two weeks, we'd sent in our online applications. I could be a Peace Corps volunteer (PCV) after all.

My memoir, *At Home On the Kazakh Steppe*, tells the story of this mid-life jump into the unknown. But it doesn't tell much about what I left behind. Somehow, writing about it felt like whining. I did, after all, join voluntarily. I did sell my Philadelphia home with the six-foot-long tub and French bidet I'd added during renovations only a few years before. I'd sold my two-year-old car for one-third of what I'd paid for it. I'd parted with furniture I loved; hundreds of books, some of them mine since high school; closets full of clothes; stuff. It was all just stuff, I reminded myself. And it still feels like whining.

Except for Merlin.

A rescued greyhound, Merlin came into our lives in August of 1999. Woody and I joke that we got married just so we could adopt him. Not my first dog by any means, but a different dog than any I'd had before. He carried himself with a graceful dignity that let us know that chasing a silly ball — never mind bringing it back just to do it again — was beneath him. He taught me patience (ever a challenge), and he was truly the world's fastest couch potato. He and I bonded quickly, and life without him was unthinkable. Until the Peace Corps entered the picture.

During the final year that it took for our medical clearance to come through, we lined up a foster home for him. But in the weeks before our departure, the family's circumstances changed and they had to renege. With two weeks to go before we were scheduled to leave, we found a second family who wanted him, but they would take him only if they could keep him. I was devastated. After forty-eight hours of angry, broken-hearted sobs, I signed him over to them permanently.

Such was the pull that becoming a PCV had on me.

Though I'd wanted to join Peace Corps for nearly forty years, by the spring of 2002, there was an even stronger pull on me to join. With the fall of the Twin Towers, Woody and I felt an unusual type of patriotism. Initially proud of the outpouring of public sympathy, even from longtime adversaries of our country, we were dismayed to find that support evaporating as our country drew closer and closer to war. We wanted to take a stand, make a statement, and be counted among those who preferred peace.

I've only mentioned the permanent losses (or what I believed at the time were permanent; we actually did get Merlin back and enjoyed him for four more years). I haven't talked about leaving behind my network of friends and colleagues, not being able to participate in two years of my grandchildren's lives, or leaving the rest of my family: the part of my life I put on hold.

Some of this was mitigated by technology: The Internet was far more available than I ever imagined it could be in a Peace Corps country. But the pain of letting go of attachments — what had, according to the Buddhist teachings I am drawn to, created my misery — did not hit me until it was too late to grab any of them back.

People often comment on how brave we were. I can see how it might look that way: Newly married, older couple abandons worldly possessions in pursuit of loftier goals. But I never felt it took any particular courage. In fact, I've come to believe that by leaving so much of what I valued behind, I was more committed to success — to "making a difference" — than I might have been otherwise, though I was never sure what that "difference" might be.

In writing my memoir, I've discovered the difference I really made was in me.

NOTE: The Peace Corps is a U.S. State Department program begun in 1961 by President John F. Kennedy. Since its beginning, it has had three goals: to provide training and skills to countries that ask for our help, to bring aspects of our culture to the people in these foreign lands, and (when we return) to teach people of the United States about these cultures.

The Peace Corps has no upper age limit and requires only that its volunteers be U.S. citizens and have either a college degree or "life experience that can be taught" (such as farming or fishing). There is a lengthy application process and a background check, and a detailed medical clearance is required. For more information, the website is www.peacecorps.gov

JANET GIVENS: Just when her life felt right — new home, new grandchildren, new career, new husband — Janet Givens left it all behind and, with her new husband, joined the Peace Corps.

Only the latest of many jumps into the unknown, her two years in the Peace Corps were filled with struggles, surprises, and rewards, vividly recalled in her memoir, *At Home on the Kazakh Steppe*, out later this year.

Fascinated with the "oh, no" moments that make us gasp, and curious about behaviors and beliefs we often take for granted, she blogs about negotiating boundaries, making connections, and embracing transitions at: www.Janetgivens.com/blog

Suellen Zima

A Hummingbird Life

UNEXPECTEDLY, BUT VERY CLEARLY, I heard myself thinking, "I know what the next 20 years of my life will be like." Immediately, and also very clearly, I heard, "But I don't want to know what the next 20 years of my life will be like." That realization didn't make much sense to me since I was living the life I had always wanted. I was in my mid-30s, happily married to my high school sweetheart, full-time mom to a healthy son, doing meaningful volunteer work, and all was well — wasn't it?

I had lived a mostly traditional lifestyle, except for consciously choosing to adopt rather than to have a biological child. I had been a foster care social worker, so it made more sense to me to take a child without a family than to create another child. We were white, and our son was black. We were a somewhat unusual family, but a happy one.

About the only thing my husband and I disagreed about was how long to go away on vacations. I loved traveling in a way he didn't. I wanted to go longer, and farther away. While my son was still a toddler, although

I had no intention of ever doing so, I signed up for a community college short course called "Traveling Alone as a Woman." What I remember most from that short course was seeing a woman who had done such a thing. A visiting guest from Israel casually mentioned that it was possible to be a volunteer on a kibbutz in Israel. I felt a shiver of excitement.

Something deep, powerful, and unrelenting inside kept pushing me out of the cozy confines of the life my husband and I had created together until, by the age of 37, I had destroyed what I spent so many years building. Our 12-year-old son, unable to feel secure with the mother I had become, chose to stay with his dad when I moved away. In the summer break from getting a master's degree in social work, I finally got to see Israel for the first time as a volunteer on a kibbutz. I was the oldest volunteer there. In 1983, at 40, I started life as an immigrant in a new land, with a new language to learn, and a new culture to decipher.

I also had chosen a new name for myself — one I fashioned from a Swahili word that incorporated my pain at leaving the husband I loved and my hope for the future. Unfortunately, I found out when I moved to Israel that it was, coincidentally, a very bad word in Hebrew.

Five years later, when my savings were down to $5,000, I thought, "I need to go around the world before I run out of money." Simple curiosity made China a priority. What I didn't expect was that China's complicated society would intrigue and magnetize me for the rest of my life.

I found that the hummingbird and I share several characteristics. We both plant our feet firmly in mid-air, hover, drink deeply, and then flit away. We are very independent creatures who live life quickly and intensely. If someone tries to hold us, we will die. But we can fly backward as well as forward at will.

I was content and, indeed, often elated living as a hummingbird throughout the world for over 16 years. Continuous new experiences challenged me. Although there were many discomforts and inconveniences, especially in third-world China, I knew I tired of the "known" much more than the "unknown." From my first teaching job in China, found by knocking on doors and saying, "Hi, I'd like to teach English," I knew I'd found my happiest career.

My journeys were geographical, but also explorations into deeply personal, emotional, and cultural dimensions. There were many truly magical moments of serendipity along the way, as well as pure luck. I am grateful I found what my soul craved. I don't have to say, "I wish I had …"

I discovered the parts that made me whole — my personality was American, my homeland was Israel, my heart was in China, and my spirit was in Bali. I turned into a sculptor of sorts, able to carve out niches for myself wherever I went. I was at home being housemother in an Israeli boarding school to newly arrived Ethiopian Jewish teenage immigrants, then living and working in an Israeli-Arab town trying to promote mutual respect between Israeli Arabs and Israeli Jews. I loved the adventure of finding teaching jobs in China, Taiwan, Macau, Bali, and Korea that allowed me inside the cultures.

From inside China, I saw the tumultuous changes in the lives of my students over more than two decades. By continually nurturing the relationships I made with my students through frequent letters and visits, I stayed in their lives, and they remain my friends today. Six of my students asked me to be the honorary grandmother to their children. Being in their children's lives as they grow up has been a continuing joy in my life.

The journals I kept as my constant traveling companions turned into my first book, *Memoirs of a Middle-aged Hummingbird*, published in 2006. The book is my link with that life that will never die.

My son never forgave me for leaving the family and refused any contact with me. However, he did re-establish contact when he knew he was dying of AIDS. He died in 2003. I recently published *Out of Step: A Diary to My Dead Son*. I have to live with a lingering guilt for having left my husband and son, but my nomadic years traveling solo to unusual nooks and crannies in the world were undoubtedly the most fulfilling years of my life.

I am now a more settled, senior hummingbird who only sometimes wanders, still wonders, and often writes.

SUELLEN ZIMA: One lucky Friday the 13th began the unusual journeys of my life as wife, mother, social worker, world explorer, English teacher, and author. My journals captured the details of my travels, published in *Memoirs of a Middle-aged Hummingbird*.

The need to make my dead son come more alive to me became a diary. *Out of Step: A Diary To My Dead Son* attempts to repair our damaged relationship by interweaving past and present, interracial adoption in the 1970s, divorce and guilt, HIV-AIDS, homosexuality, and one mother-son relationship. I continue to wander, wonder, and blog as *The Senior Hummingbird*. Website: www.zimatravels.com/

Terri Elders

A HAPPY HEART

"So what do you do?"

In the '70s when strangers at parties asked this, I could have fudged … just say I worked for the county and leave it at that. Instead, I'd provide a flat-out conversation-stopper.

"I'm the psychiatric social worker for MacLaren Hall's nursery," I'd answer. "That's where neglected and abused kids await court disposition. I do play therapy with the toddlers and try to get help for their abusing parents."

I'd smile and wait. People usually inched away, as if I'd confided that I ran pigeon drop scams on senior citizens. Or that I might be contagious.

During the ensuing silence, I'd watch eyes glaze and jaws drop.

"Oh," they'd sputter, "I couldn't do that." They'd nod and sidle off in search of someone with a more socially redeeming occupation.

Burnout rates soar in my profession. Social workers, like police, rarely get thanked. Instead, they're criticized by the very people they strive to aid, and vilified by the press and the general public for not doing enough.

I didn't expect accolades, parades, or even sympathetic ears from strangers at parties. Nobody wants to hear about babies who've been abandoned in garbage bins or children who've been tortured. I understood that, so I didn't tell horror stories.

If anybody stuck around long enough, I could relate sunny tales. Many addicted parents I'd counseled successfully completed rehab, found jobs, and visited their children in foster care. I could mention the four-year-old voluntary mute who spoke again as we manipulated finger puppets.

In earlier days, my husband, Bob, a policeman, listened patiently when I vented. With an equally stress-filled job, he empathized. Over the years, though, he'd sought relief in vodka, eventually spiraling downward into alcoholism. He'd been in several outpatient programs, and on and off the wagon, but nothing took. I'd occasionally think of divorce, but I'd shove that troubling notion aside. *He needs me*, I'd convince myself.

Not long before I started at MacLaren, Bob entered an inpatient program. This one worked. With a commitment to sobriety, he no longer was around to give me emotional support. He spent every free minute in Twelve Step meetings and hospital aftercare programs.

I needed to find support elsewhere. I recognized that some of my colleagues already suffered from compassion fatigue, burnout, and depression. Some coped by eating compulsively or relying on tranquilizers. I wanted to continue with my job, but I certainly didn't want to pack on unneeded pounds, float through my days like a zombie, or eventually be diagnosed with post-traumatic stress disorder.

I started to frequent an art gallery that published a magazine. I wrote articles for it, and made friends who were artists, photographers, and poets. I enrolled in an aerobic dance class and lost myself in choreographed routines, pretending to be a Broadway chorine.

Despite these distractions, my marriage continued to unravel. One day, toweling off after a particularly invigorating aerobics session, I noticed my heartbeat seemed to stutter. By the time I got dressed, it beat normally again. I forgot about it until one day at work when I broke out in a cold sweat. The stutter had returned.

I saw my doctor, who gave me an electrocardiogram.

"You're experiencing premature ventricular contractions, commonly called PVCs," she explained. "It's not dangerous yet, but it could be. What's going on in your life?"

"My husband and I may be headed for divorce," I confessed. "I worry about that, and about the children I work with. I try to take care of myself. I go to aerobics three times a week but drink a lot of coffee."

"Caffeine, too much exercise, a high-stress job, plus anxiety over your marriage all could be contributing factors," she said. "The sooner you make decisions, the better you'll be. Not knowing one way or another how a marriage or a job will work out adds to your stress. Rid yourself of uncertainty. Don't be afraid to take the first step."

Bob resented my new activities, preferring that I devote my free time to accompanying him to recovery meetings. Delighted with his progress, I still didn't want my life to revolve around his sobriety, as it had around his drinking. I wanted to write and dance.

That issue resolved itself after Bob confessed he'd fallen in love with one of his outpatient counselors. We agreed to separate.

I continued working at MacLaren through one administrative upheaval after another. I'd think about leaving for a job with more regular hours, one that wouldn't require me to work on Sundays. But I'd remember the children. *They need me,* I reasoned.

Then one afternoon, after I learned that my play therapy room would be converted into an additional dormitory, I felt my heart skip a beat again.

The arrhythmia was back, but this time I knew what to do. Not burned out yet, but scenting smoke. Even though I'd invested 15 years in county employment, a future retirement pension wouldn't keep my heart healthy today.

I updated my resume, sent out applications and, within months, landed a new job in the private sector with an HMO. Not perfect, but a change. And my happier heart calmed down permanently.

It's been over 25 years now since I've experienced any arrhythmia. It's not as if I've led a stress-free life. I've worked overseas with the Peace Corps and held other demanding jobs. I remarried and saw my second husband through a long series of illnesses and eventual hospice care.

I do the routine things: keep caffeine to a minimum, exercise reasonably, and get enough sleep.

But my real secret is that I don't remain immersed in uncertainty. I don't allow myself to feel trapped by the perceived needs of others. I seek a way to take that first step. After all, I need my heart to live. I owe myself good health.

Now when people ask me what I do, I have a favorite response. It raises eyebrows.

"I keep a happy heart," I say.

TERRI ELDERS, LCSW, lives near Colville, Washington, with two dogs and three cats. Terri is a lifelong writer and editor whose stories have appeared in dozens of periodicals and anthologies, including multiple editions of *Not Your Mother's Book, Dream of Things, Chicken Soup for the Soul, A Cup of Comfort, Patchwork Path, Thin Threads, Tending Your Inner Garden,* and *God Makes Lemonade*. She is the in-house copy editor for Publishing Syndicate, and co-creator of its anthology, *Not Your Mother's Book: On Travel*. Website: www.Atouchoftarragon.blogspot.com

Jan Marshall

IN THE BEGINNING, they claimed they never promised us a rose garden. Never said there *wasn't* one, so I assumed I'd wake up and bees
would be a buzzin'.

Then someone up there said, "Hey, lady, wanna learn some great
lessons?" Before I could answer, like everyone else in some manner,
I endured grief, disappointments, illness including cancer and, more
recently, brain surgery, plus some bad fish.

Fortunately, I have a congenital condition known as Opticockyitis,
named after the doctor who diagnosed it in a cocker spaniel. It's an
affliction causing me to observe most situations a bit off center. Can't
help myself. It is like being born with a Whoopee cushion in my head.
Whenever I was dealt a major blow in life, and **after** I finished crying,
moaning, and complaining, my ability to observe the moment with this
unusual perspective *saved* my life, according to my physicians.

But I have a confession to make. After first being touched by an angel in an inappropriate place, I was shocked. "Not me, not cancer." I had mammograms every year, ate well, jogged, practiced yoga, laughed, and made love frequently (sometimes at the same time — talk about multitasking or attention deficit disorder) so, *of course*, I *had* to be immune.

As a motivational seminar leader teaching about the connection between mind and body, I stressed the need for humor. In my workshops I taught that increasing the *laughter* in one's life is essential to one's wellbeing. I was a newspaper *humor* columnist and an author of *funny survival* books. I was founder of the International Humor & Healing Institute and a certified master clinical hypnotherapist. How could this have happened?

No one in my family had had cancer. I did not fit any statistics: oh yeah, except the part about early detection. My trusted radiologist made a major error: He hadn't noticed the cancer during the last few mammograms in the fourteen years he was my doctor. *Oops!*

The situation became worse with every decision. Before the cancer and lousy chemotherapy, I was a healthy lady. Cancer can make you sick; not the illness itself, but the treatment. Years ago, *though not now,* receiving chemotherapy was like dropping a bomb to catch a fly; killing the insect, but affecting so much more.

I believe in fifty years we will think that placing toxins in our bodies is barbaric.

People will say, "You're kidding. Do you mean in the twentieth century when people had a severe illness, they removed the part with the problem and then they pumped your body full of crap? *Eeew!*"

When told I needed a biopsy I asked whether it mattered if I waited a couple of weeks. I had a scheduled speaking engagement in Washington, D.C., plus a meeting with Patch Adams, that remarkable physician who uses humor in dealing with his patients and dreamed of building a free hospital.

We shared information. I told him about my plan for placing humor/healing rooms in hospitals to start, then in corporations and schools.

I had designed rooms to promote healing by inducing positive emotions in a hospital setting in conjunction with other medical therapies. It was intended to prevent burnout among staff and as a pleasant waiting section for visitors. These areas would feature healing colors, soothing sound, ergonomically designed furniture, and humor from every medium, so enlightened physicians could write a prescription for the patient to spend time in the Humor Room just as they would prescribe any other physical therapy.

The first place was to be the "Steve Allen Humor Room." Steve had become a dear friend and supporter after he appeared on my television show, and I was a frequent guest on his syndicated WNEW radio program. He was a kind, brilliant, and funny man.

The doctor said it would be OK to take my trip if I agreed not to wait more than those two weeks. I took healing tapes to play in my hotel room as well as books and soothing meditations. I knew I'd be OK. I have always believed in the power of prayer and the kindness of strangers. "Not so fast," Grandma used to say. "Man plans. God laughs hysterically."

It *was* cancer. It had spread to lymph nodes.

I had chemotherapy and, much later, brain tumor surgery. When my hair grew back an inch, just for fun my caregiver dyed it blond for two days.

I looked like rocker Eminem, cursed, and grabbed my crotch a lot. I let it grow back auburn.

I was no longer recognizable to myself. I cried in the shower every day. After the screams and unending tears, a new plan was necessary: to do what had always helped me before, which was to get out of *me* and assist others.

I had done that when Steve Allen died suddenly, and my grief was so enormous that I gave up dreams of installing Humor Rooms.

Whenever I am in a funk, what often helps me (besides music or funny films) is helping someone else out of his or her distress.

So I presented university programs regarding the benefits of humor in business, which were voted the best for three years in a row, and I shared healing techniques with doctors, nurses, and technicians at clinics, hospitals, and major corporations.

But the two actions that proved most helpful to me were: 1) forming "Jan's Army" and awarding badges of heroism to other survivors and 2) keeping notes and seeking out the humor in daily hassles, such as dealing with new technology, Internet dating, and more; then turning them into newspaper columns and books, the most recent: *Dancin', Schmancin' with the Scars: Finding the Humor No Matter What!* (Dancin' is code for anything pleasurable.)

It is dedicated to veterans, cancer and brain tumor survivors, and regular people simply dealing with "stuff." Most important, it includes tips and techniques for living joyfully, even when going through a rough patch.

I'm still "dancin'" — as are all you gutsy people, even though *your very own* scars may not be visible. Cheers to you!

JAN MARSHALL is the cheeky, very *seasoned* humorologist and author of satirical survival books. Her most recent, *Dancin', Schmancin With the Scars: Finding the Humor No Matter What!* is available through Amazon and on ebook devices.

A newspaper columnist and media humorist, Jan hosted her own television series and is a national speaker and consultant.

The International Humor & Healing Institute, which she founded in 1986, included among other board members Norman Cousins, Dr. Bernie Siegel, John Cleese, and Steve Allen. Jan is a certified master clinical hypnotherapist. Website: www.authorjanmarshall.com

Joe Weddington

THE UNSEEN BULLET

JOIN THE ARMY, SEE THE WORLD. That is what I did. I signed up for the infantry as long as the army would send me to Europe, pay for me to finish college, and give me some money.

Basic training and infantry training were almost a joke to me as a multi-sports athlete, but I tolerated the near-comical antics of the drill sergeants, as I knew they had to bring younger boys up to speed while keeping the attention of more worldly fellows like myself. I was 24 and had traveled a bit by then, had worked a job or two, had three years of college behind me, and had even run my own business. My friends thought I was crazy for enlisting, but I did it.

Arriving in Germany and assigned to a unit, I did my job and spent my free time on the rails, seeing every country I could see from The Netherlands to Italy to France and all points in between. I took college classes at the Education Center on post and lucked in to driving a staff officer who traveled widely and regularly. My life was on track.

Then I was sent to Iraq and went to war. Over a short period of time, I became completely desensitized to death, both as a reality and as a concept, not shedding a single tear at the funeral of my own mother a year later. I finished school, left the army for the reserves, earned my pilot's license, got married, went to work, moved into my childhood home in a great neighborhood, had children, and led an active life. I was a football coach, a pilot and squadron commander in the Civil Air Patrol, volunteered for emergency services, and ran a successful appraisal and home inspection office.

Two years after I came home I began having problems with short-term memory, and my limbs would jerk for no reason, throwing me into bouts of severe cramping all over my body. My legs began to swell notably, and I gained 200 pounds over about five years. One day at work my legs began to feel as if they were on fire. They were swelling rapidly, to such a degree that they split open, leaking fluid and blood. I was rushed to the hospital, where I contracted a methicillin-resistant Staphylococcus aureus infection and suffered its damaging effects.

I was in organ failure and fighting for my life when doctors discovered scar tissue on my brain. It seemed my proximity to a mortar detonation that had thrown me headfirst into the wheel of a Hummer had done more than just addle me at the time. My other symptoms were attributed to pyridostigmine bromide (PB) pills the army issued to protect soldiers against exposure to nerve gas agents, depleted uranium, and other/unknown toxins. I had effectively been badly wounded by a silent bullet and didn't even know it.

I lived, my symptoms in check but uncured. I left the hospital with permanent nerve damage, deformed and discolored legs, and pain that I will have to live with for the rest of my life. I had a later bout with a blood clot in my leg going to my lungs and spent several days in a coma. I became depressed and lethargic, with regular thoughts of suicide. I was no longer the man I had been. After fifteen years of marriage, my wife left me for a man half her age. At 40 years old, I lost my kids, I lost my business, I lost my home. I lost everything.

Now I am 48. I live in a trailer that I have made into a home using many items from the old house to do so. It is a comfort to the kids that something of their past is preserved and comfortably familiar to me. I drive a dependable, 15-year-old SUV; I take my medicine; and I go to doctors' appointments, physical therapy, and meetings with my lawyer to increase my VA benefits. I take a dozen pills a day for my symptoms. I receive $680 per month from a 100 percent Social Security disability for post-traumatic stress disorder and other symptoms, and $640 from the VA, which refuses to acknowledge what has happened to me and rates me at 40 percent disability for "combat anxiety" and "tinnitus." I manage a few hundred dollars from other sources. A far cry from the $1,000-plus-a-week take-home I had become accustomed to.

I get by, though. I have learned to watch every expense and still manage to go to the movies with my son now and then, and to dine out with both him and his sister once a month. I add to things by picking up cans and collecting scrap metal and am fortunate to have a sister who helps me out often with unexpected bills. Vacations are rare, but I still manage to take one on occasion. Until recently, I was embarrassed to wear shorts in public until this pretty young waitress said to me, "Hey, they are your legs, the only ones you have got, don't worry about it." I have worn shorts every day since. Life changed for me, but life goes on and I recently became a grandfather. Life is good.

JOE WEDDINGTON's dad was a businessman, former professional baseball player, and World War II veteran of the Marines. His mom was a lifelong homemaker. Joe grew up in the Mayberry-like town of Prestonsburg, Kentucky. He owned his first business, an excavation company, at age 16. Joe worked in South Florida as a crane truck driver and operator before joining the U.S. Army infantry and serving in combat in Desert Storm. A number of service-related ailments hastened his divorce and forced him into disability retirement. He just became a grandfather. www.facebook.com/joedweddington

Mayu Molina Lehmann

WRITING IN A SECOND LANGUAGE

I RECENTLY READ A PIECE in *The New York Times* by Mr. Corstica Bradatan, a Bulgarian writer. Having moved from Bulgaria to the U.S., he talks about the difficulty of finding a voice in a new language:

> *"When you become a writer, you don't do so in abstract, but in relation to a certain language. To practice writing is to grow roots into that language; the better writer you become, the deeper the roots. Literary virtuosity almost always betrays a sense of deep, comfortable immersion into familiar soil. As such, if for any reason the writer has to change languages, the experience is nothing short of life-threatening."*

I understand this feeling completely: Growing up in Mexico, I was passionate about the Spanish language. I have loved reading ever since I can remember, and I started writing short stories when I was seven years old.

One of the best traditions of my childhood was that every year, my dad would take me to the International Book Fair in Mexico City. We would spend the whole day combing the aisles, exchanging books, excited at our findings. We would then emerge from the fair carrying a heavy box of books, exhausted but happy, satisfied with our treasures. It is one of the happiest memories of my childhood.

My love for books never dimmed, and when the time came to choose a course of study for a bachelor's degree, I chose Spanish literature without hesitation. Then, for four glorious years, I immersed myself in the richness of the language, from the works of the Middle Ages to the classics of the Spanish Golden Age to the most recent emergence of Latin-American writers. I loved every part of it.

I pride myself for knowing how to write well, knowing by heart the intricacies of the accentuation and conjugation, based on the Royal Academy of the Spanish Language. During those years I took an elective course, Latin, and was filled with delight when I learned the origin of a word. It was like polishing a word as though it were a gem, and discovering what it was made of.

Since I loved writing, I thought I could make a name for myself as a writer. I wrote a novel, a couple of scripts for theater, and short stories. I never thought of living outside the Spanish world that I so loved. It never occurred to me to be separated from my beloved linguistic universe.

But fate had other plans, and ironically, I somehow ended up living in the capital of the United States, where my literary references were put out of context. Even though I spoke English, I was not fully comfortable with it. I was, as Bradatan explains, devoid of a language:

> *"When changing languages you descend to a zero-point of your existence. There must be even a moment, however brief, when you cease to be. You've quit the old language and the new one hasn't received you yet; you are now in limbo, between worlds, hanging over the abyss."*

And hanging over the abyss I was, in the middle of an English-speaking country, equipped with a deep knowledge of a language that amounted to little here. Other than Shakespeare and Hemingway, I had no reference to writers of the English language. I was in a void. I was in limbo.

Then, two or three years after I had moved to the US, my brother Alfonso, who is a musician, approached me with the idea of writing a musical. He would write the music; I would write the script. I jumped enthusiastically at the idea, and we started working right away. We both agreed it should be in English. I was intimidated at first, but eventually I jumped into the unknown ... writing in English for the first time.

Although scary at first, the experience proved to be incredibly liberating. Writing in Spanish had carried a lot of gravitas, to the point of being paralyzing. I had such respect for the language that I feared disappointing the great masters. *What would Cervantes think of this?* I would ask myself in anguish. By contrast, my lack of knowledge of English literature allowed me to write more freely, without imagining anyone looking over my shoulder. I found out that writing in English gave me the bliss of ignorance.

I finished the script and went on to write short stories and memoir pieces for my two girls. I surprised myself by choosing English to do so. Again as the Bulgarian writer says: *"To abandon your native tongue and to adopt another is to dismantle yourself, piece by piece, and then put yourself together again, in a different form."*

That was exactly me, forced to look at what I knew, dissect it, discard some things, hold on to some and put everything back together in a way that was still me, but a little different. For example, literary embellishments and excessive adjectives don't go well in English, so writing in this language forced me to see the world through different eyes, in a more objective and matter-of-fact way. The result was a new way of writing, made of bits and pieces of the old me, plus elements of my new environment.

As Bradatan observes:

> *"In the end, you don't really change languages;*
> *the language changes you."*

In my case, it did.

MAYU MOLINA LEHMANN was born and raised in Sonora, Mexico. Developing an early love for literature, she wrote her first story at age seven. The anthology *De Niños Para Niños* (Ediciones del Plumicornio) includes some of her earlier works. She authored an unpublished novel, *La Hija del Candidato,* and is writing the script for a musical about Latino immigration.

Mayu has a BA in Spanish literature from Tec de Monterrey (ITESM). After moving to the U.S. she worked at the Organization for American States in Washington, D.C., where she currently lives with her husband and two young daughters. Website: www.mayuswords.blogspot.com/

Cappy Hall Rearick

To Have and Have Not

"You got to know when to hold 'em, know when to fold 'em,
Know when to walk away and know when to run."
—Kenny Rogers

ACT ONE.

We walked around the block over and over, my best friend and I. She tried to talk me out of leaving my husband; I didn't want to listen. I was stuck in emotional quicksand.

"Stop walking and stop talking, Lynn," I said. "I have to do this because I don't know who I am anymore."

She heard the truth of my words. After only a moment of looking into my soul, she wrapped me in her arms. "Then go with God."

I can't say that it was God riding with me as I drove away from the small town where I had lived with my little family for a decade, but there was a force of some kind. It propelled me back to my other nest, the one built by my parents.

Leaving behind a stifling marriage that had stolen my identity consumed me with both relief and fear. While on the one hand I felt liberated, rock-bottom grief for leaving my two young sons behind chewed up pieces of my heart and spit them out. I cried and cried and cried.

As though my mind was in instant replay, I saw the eyes of my twelve-year-old boy, who was holding himself together as though following instructions. Even at his age, he knew there was nothing he could do to stop me from going. Being the oldest, he must have told himself to be brave since his mother couldn't show him how to behave. The longer and harder I hugged him, the more stoic he became. So like his father.

In my mind, I saw my youngest son, my baby. How does one tell a nine-year-old that his life is about to change and will never be the same? I held him in my lap and rocked him like I did when he really was a baby. We both wept. I kissed his face and tasted his tears, not realizing that it might be the last time he would let me hold him close or cry with him.

The year was 1973. I lived in the Deep South, where motherhood and apple pie were the benchmarks to which young women aspired. Divorce that allowed a husband to raise the children was not in that equation. With the exception of my friend Lynn, who grasped my situation like only a good friend can, no one understood my decision.

My mother had suspected my unhappiness, but it was hard for her to empathize. She gave me a safe harbor, but she could not own my broken heart or my shattered spirit.

I was thirty-three years old and, as I look back all these years later, I am troubled by the serious errors in judgment I made. I was so tired, so lost that I didn't consider the long-range emotional fallout destined to haunt both my children and me for the rest of our lives.

Strange as it may seem, Husband Number One and I parted on fairly good terms. We were civilized about things; he promised to keep me in the loop regarding the boys, and he did.

Not long after we separated, he told me how they cried for me at night, and how valiantly they were coping in a world that had left them bereft. I so wished he had not told me. Even after all these years, I still hear my babies crying when I lay my own head on the pillow at night. I will hear them till the day I die.

I moved to where I had attended college because it was familiar territory, even though I no longer knew anyone there. Because I lived alone, separation anxiety was my companion. The grief I felt for my children ached like a phantom limb; I missed being their mother and easily convinced myself that they would hate me. That thought brought me to my knees again and again.

At night I would grab the telephone to call them and then quickly change my mind, afraid that they would say they no longer wanted me in their lives. Emotionally, I never left my boys, but I was scared to death that they believed I had abandoned them the day I left their father. I was also afraid of an opposite reaction. Would hearing my voice make it harder for them to adjust to the life they had not chosen? Did I dare risk heaping even more emotional stress onto my innocent children? I so wanted what was best for them.

In the end, I would call Dial a Prayer so that I could hear the sound of a human voice, albeit a recorded one.

Many years and a boatload of heartache and change would have to take place before I could begin to feel whole again, although a part of my sad heart will always remain broken. I was a mother who left her children, so my lifeboat was filled with guilt.

My sons grew up to be fine men and, remarkably, my worry of not being loved by them materialized *only* in my fear-drenched mind. They have made me immeasurably proud by becoming better parents than I could ever have been. Their children are sweet and good, and I am blessed that they, too, have allowed me to be part of their lives.

I had to leave the life I was living in 1973 because it no longer worked, and I didn't have a clue how to fix things. At the time, I didn't know what my future held or if I deserved to have one. Driving out of town that day forty years ago, I wasn't even sure I deserved a future.

As it turned out, Act Two was waiting in the wings.

CAPPY HALL REARICK: Syndicated humor columnist Cappy Hall Rearick has authored six columns: *Alive and Well in Hollywood, Tidings, Simply Southern, Simply Senior, Puttin' On The Gritz,* and a monthly e-column, *Simply Something.*

She has six published books in print: *Simply Southern, Simply Southern Ease, Simply Christmas, Return to Rocky Bottom, The Road to Hell is Seldom Seen* and *I Do, I Do, I Do.* A regular contributor to *Not Your Mother's Book* series, her work can be found in anthologies throughout the country. Cappy and husband Bill live on St. Simons Island, Georgia, and Saluda, North Carolina. Website: www.simplysoutherncappy.com

Don Westenhaver

Team Building Is Not for the Faint of Heart

I SPENT ALMOST 40 YEARS working for big corporations. The pay was great, but the work was high-pressure and demanding. With thousands of employees to manage, department heads had to work closely with each other. This led to a ridiculous set of exercises named Team Building.

In 1991 I had been promoted into an executive position just in time to attend a three-day exercise in Warner Hot Springs, which was so far from civilization that the rustic hotel rooms had no televisions. I was so nervous about the event I felt nauseous. A born introvert, I was always intimidated by social situations where I was surrounded by semi-strangers talking about sports. But this was serious. If I made an idiot of myself at this event, all the company big shots would forever remember my foolishness as their first impression of me.

Early in the morning, we met in a conference room. There were about 30 of us — 29 men and one woman. They all seemed to know each other but looked at me as though I were painted green. A team-building consultant led the first exercise with an introductory speech as we sat around one large table. He held a tennis ball in his hand.

"I am going to throw this ball at one of you. This person will then throw it to another person and then say something nice about that person. That person will then pick someone else to throw the ball to and say something nice about that person. And so on."

You already know where this is heading, don't you? The most popular guys were chosen first. Being a stranger, I was the second to last person to receive the ball. I had to throw it to the last person and say something nice about him. This was a challenge. If he had had some virtue, he already would have been picked. I can't remember what I said. Maybe I just passed out.

Next the consultant led us outside and grabbed a hula hoop. We all had to stand in a circle holding hands. I hate holding hands, especially with other men. The consultant broke the circle for a moment to insert the hula hoop around one person's arm.

"Now I want you to work this hula hoop around this circle without letting go of your neighbors' hands. Step through the hoop with your legs and loop it over your head to the next person." This was just plain silly, but at least I survived it without losing my balance and falling over.

For the rest of the day we were broken into five teams that competed with each other. A vice president was put in charge of each team, and they took turns choosing their team members. You all remember how humiliating this was in grammar school? Being the last one chosen? Well, it's even worse when you're in your 40s.

The five teams played problem-solving games. For example, we were given a few planks of wood and some bricks and told to use them to cross a pond. It would be easy with enough wood and bricks, but there weren't enough, so we had to be creative — to "think outside the box." Almost all executives are "Type A" personalities: driven, self-confident, and aggressive. So each person thought he had the best plan, and we had to debate which plan was best. Just like with a real business problem.

Another example was to climb a 12-foot fence without a ladder. We had to lift a guy to the top, then he pulled another guy up, etc. I started enjoying the events. A handful of us had fought in Vietnam, giving us a common history to bond over. We remarked about how some of the games had parallels in combat operations.

Now part of a six-man team instead of the initial 30-person mob, I felt more confident. In each game I tossed out a suggestion or two about overcoming the obstacles. The other five guys listened and nodded, which encouraged me to continue to speak up.

On the second day, we got to climb trees. It was a day I will never forget. We took turns strapping ourselves into harnesses hooked to ropes and pulleys, and then climbing to a platform on top of a 50-foot tree. The objective was to jump off the platform and grab a trapeze bar. Of course, if I missed the bar, I'd be saved by the harness, assuming I did not swing face first into a tree. I loved it!

Some of the games were done in pairs, and we were matched up by weight. As one of the smallest men, I was matched up with the lone woman, which was fine.

All day we were like kids again, swinging across water with ropes, diving into trampolines, playing tug-of-war, and racing across tree limbs. The grand finale was to walk across a four-inch beam between two trees, high in the air — with a harness, of course. The consultant asked for volunteers to try it blindfolded. I shouted out "I'll do it!" and the next thing I knew, I was a circus performer. I made it all the way across with no problem, to the cheers of the group.

That evening over drinks we all told stories of our victories, and I finally felt like I belonged.

DON WESTENHAVER served with the Marines in Vietnam as a radioman and interpreter. His fascination with different cultures grew with many visits to Asia, Europe, Latin America, and Africa as a finance executive. These experiences inspired his first two novels, *The Whiplash Hypothesis* and

The Red Turtle Project. Don's third and fourth novels, *Nero's Concert* and *Alexander's Lighthouse*, spring from his lifelong interest in ancient Rome, backed up by intense research and many travels.

Don and his wife assist with three different charities, play golf, read novels, and love to travel. They are blessed with two daughters and two grandchildren. His website is: www.don westenhaver.com

Lola Di Giulio De Maci

The Beginning of Tomorrow

I HAD ALWAYS WANTED TO go back to school. And one day, thirty years later, I did. I don't know what gave me the guts to do it other than a burning desire to finish something I had started years ago. When the day came to register, I was terrified and got "cold feet."

"I decided that I'm not going back to school," I told my family. "I don't really want this after all. I'm going to forget about it."

My daughter, who was a freshman in college at the time, sensed my apprehension. "Mom," she said pleadingly, "you've wanted to do this all your life. I'll go with you to register; I'll even stand in line for you." And she did.

I had dropped out of college in my senior year, and now it was like starting all over again. But I didn't know where to start. As chance would have it, in one of the first textbooks I opened as "an older returning student," I came across a quote by Lewis Carroll from *Alice in Wonderland* and *Through the Looking Glass*: "Begin at the beginning," the King said gravely, "and go on till you come to the end; then stop." My sentiments exactly, Mr. Carroll. Thank you.

But it had been a long time since I had "cracked a book." I studied sometimes eight hours a day, forgetting to eat lunch or feed the goldfish. My husband and I would have to make dates in order to see one another, and at times I felt guilty for choosing to spend an hour in the library and then having to make dinner from a box.

When graduation day finally arrived, I was ecstatic. Not only was I fulfilling a lifelong dream, but my daughter was also graduating — on the same day. We had a mother-daughter celebration with family and friends, proudly displaying our newly acquired bachelor of arts degrees. I have never been so proud of my daughter. And when my daughter stood next to me at picture-taking time, our black robes blending into one, I could tell that she was very proud of her mother.

Shortly after graduation, I attained a teaching credential. And because I loved to learn and found teaching to be one of the best avenues to learning, I decided to continue my studies and go for a master of arts degree in education and creative writing. It was an excellent choice. I loved teaching, and I loved writing. And with a degree in interdisciplinary studies, I could combine the two.

Graduate school was exhausting and overwhelming at times. I cut my hair short and got the first permanent of my life so that I wouldn't have to bother with setting my hair ... and I found out that I could live without my nightly rendezvous with Ted Danson from "Cheers."

The next two years flew by, but it wasn't easy. At one point, I came home from school, threw my books on the kitchen counter, and announced: "I'm quitting! I've had it!" After crying for a couple of hours and talking it over with my family, I realized that I had come too far to quit. I had run the race well, and I was tired. I decided I would take one day at a time, resting on the sidelines.

I was in my final quarter of graduate school with only one class left to take when I found out I had cancer. Cancer. Was I going to die? Would I have to leave my children so soon? Would I be able to finish school?

A couple of days later, shaken and apprehensive, I appeared at my professor's door, leaving a puddle of tears and broken dreams on his shoulders. "Don't worry about it," he said. "We can work something out."

"But I have to go to Los Angeles for seven weeks of radiation therapy and won't be able to come to class." He suggested that I do my work in Los Angeles and send it to him through the mail. We could keep in touch by telephone.

"And don't give up," he said adamantly. "I have never met a student with so much determination. You are the kind of student teachers come to school for. And you have to use that same determination to fight this thing."

I promised him I would finish my schoolwork, and I would fight for my life. The kitchen table in my apartment in Los Angeles became my desk for the next seven weeks. I would go for my treatment and return to my apartment to study and write my papers. I mailed my completed assignments from a post office nearby.

Right before Christmas, I graduated with honors with a master of arts degree in education and English. My graduation day was special for a lot of reasons. I had finished my radiation treatments and my schoolwork. My husband and my children, along with my mother, sister, and brother, were in the audience of the auditorium when they called my name and handed me my diploma. My eyes met their eyes and I wanted to shout, "Hey! Look at me! I did it!" And after I passed my tassel from the right side of my cap to the left, I waved to them as though I were royalty. Queen Elizabeth had nothing on me!

As I write this piece, I am eighteen years free of breast cancer. I take each day and live it, celebrating the miracle of each brand-new morning.

Over the years I have had the privilege of teaching many children and have lived to see them doing great things with their lives. And best of all, I have lived to see my daughter become a teacher and my son, a psychologist. Talk about pride!

And in my quiet times, I write — something I've loved to do since I was a child.

Life doesn't get much better than this.

LOLA Di GIULIO De MACI lives in Southern California, where she gathers inspiration for her stories, which appear in *The Ultimate Series, Tending Your Inner Garden,* the Kids' Reading Room of the *Los Angeles Times,* and in several editions of *Chicken Soup for the Soul.* Lola realized her dream when she graduated with her bachelor's degree at age 51 and a master's degree at 55. A retired teacher, she continues writing from her loft overlooking the San Bernardino Mountains. Contact her at: LDeMaci@aol.com.

Ed Robinson

A LEAP OF FAITH

M Y WIFE AND I FOUND OURSELVES discontented. We had good jobs, a strong marriage, and an all-around decent, middle-class American life. Somehow it wasn't enough. We decided to make a change, a really big change.

We decided to quit our jobs and run away to paradise to live on a boat. At first it was a crazy dream. Later, as we planned and took real steps to make it happen, it became a possibility. Eventually we made our dream come true.

How did we do it? What steps did we take? First we tackled our debt. We continued working hard and made it our life's goal to eliminate all of our debt. It took several years of dedication, but we finally managed to rid ourselves of every single debt we had. What a feeling!

Next we saved money. Without a car payment or credit card bills, this was not so hard. We simply kept on living at the same comfort level we previously enjoyed, but put all the now freed-up cash into savings. We maxed out our 401(k) plan contributions. We put every spare cent in the bank.

Along the way we learned to stop buying things we didn't need. We simply quit buying anything new unless we could eat it, drink it, or wipe our butts with it. We started donating clothing to Goodwill. As our load lightened, we started to feel unburdened. It was then that we made the decision to get rid of *everything*. That's right, we sold or gave away everything we owned, except some clothing, our laptop, and a few mementos we couldn't part with.

One day we decided we had had enough of the "work till you die world," and we quit the rat race. We loaded our meager remaining belongings into our pickup truck and headed south on I-95 for Florida. Did we have enough money saved to carry us for the rest of our lives? Nope. Did we have enough to hold us over until we reached Social Security age? Probably not. What did we have? We had enough to buy a decent boat and enough to live on for several years. We called it our Leap Of Faith. We were going to live for today. Tomorrow? Who knows?

Oh, what a feeling of freedom we enjoyed driving south. We had no job to report to. We had no bills to pay. Of course, we had no home, either, but that didn't matter to us. We were only looking ahead. We landed in Punta Gorda, Florida, on January 3, 2010. We rented a condo for a month while we boat shopped. Soon we settled on a gorgeous classic trawler, laid our money down, and moved aboard. We named our new home Leap Of Faith.

After a getting-acquainted period, we threw the lines, left the marina, and set off to explore the west coast of Florida. We lived at anchor, mostly off uninhabited islands. We became one with nature. We made friends with the dolphins and manatees. We staked claim to our own personal beach. Every night we celebrated the sunset. Every night we slept the sleep of the contented.

Once we got our sea legs, we began to travel. We cruised to the Keys, hopping from island to island until we landed in Key West.

We cruised north, falling in love with Longboat Key and the Manatee River. The place we called home was Pelican Bay, a pristine cove tucked between the islands of Cayo Costa and Punta Blanca. We would spend months isolated from society, returning only occasionally to re-provision. Our love for each other deepened dramatically. We learned so much about each other. We also learned to appreciate the silence. We slowed our pace and took in the beauty of nature. We discovered our Eden in Pelican Bay.

Our blood pressure lowered. Our heart rates slowed. Time itself slowed down for us. We lost weight. We felt healthier. We felt happier. We were so damn happy, sometimes we would just sit and laugh at our good fortune. We still feel that way today.

Money? Yes, we still had to spend some. Food, fuel, boat maintenance, and repairs all added up. Two major boat repairs took a big chunk of what was left of our savings. We lasted three years before we started to get nervous about how little money we had left. I constantly reassured my wife, "It will work out." Soon enough we returned to civilization. I wrote a book that is selling moderately well at Amazon. I also picked up a part-time job at the marina. My wife is waiting tables in town. I've written a second book, and we are starting to rebuild our bank account.

We have absolutely no regrets. We've got egrets, but no regrets. What will we do when the bank account gets big enough? Take off again, of course!

ED ROBINSON was a reporter and editor of a weekly newspaper, *The Smyrna Times*. He was also a contributing writer for *The Mariner Magazine*, a Maryland-based publication covering all things boating and fishing. After twenty years working for a major utility, he quit his job and moved onto a boat. He and his wife, Kim, are somewhere on the west coast of Florida.

His book *Leap Of Faith: Quit Your Job And Live On A Boat* is currently a best seller at Amazon.com. Website: www.strikingly .com/ed-robinson-7146

Boyd Lemon

To Live Life, I Cannot Fear Change

A T AGE 66 I HAD LIVED MY whole life in California, most of it on the coast, where the difference between summer and winter is about ten degrees. Some might consider such a climate ideal, and I suppose it is, but I yearned to experience the four seasons. I decided, if not now, when?

I sold my house, and I sold, gave away, or stored most of my possessions, including my car. I rented an apartment in the Back Bay of Boston, sight unseen, and shipped my remaining possessions before I got on a plane. Then, feeling the rush of freedom, I said goodbye to California.

On the plane, a red-eye, I knew before the wheels left the ground that I wouldn't sleep. My mind and body were overflowing with that combination of excitement and fear that took me to the precipice of dysfunction. I labored through those feelings with a firsthand understanding of the workings of human emotion I had recently read about — that fear and excitement result in the same activity within the brain. I feared the cold weather that this California boy had never experienced, the loneliness of knowing only one person in a strange city, and a culture that I knew was far different from California.

Upon stepping out of the taxi in front of my apartment building, I slipped on the ice and fell on my ass. Welcome to Boston.

A few days later I awoke at first light, sat up, and looked out the window. The world was white. Sheets of snow blew diagonally by my window. My first nor'easter in all its fierceness had been blowing its ice and snow through the night. No sidewalk or street showed through. I could barely make out the top of the yellow fireplug two stories below. Some undeciphered perversity in me wanted to get out there. I dressed while coffee was brewing. After savoring the aroma and taste of the warm coffee sweetened with lots of Stevia, I was even more antsy to get out. This was the real East Coast, never before experienced by this California boy. Genuine Boston. On top of my regular clothes, I donned my Red Sox sweatshirt, jeans — I already had on long underwear — and wool socks, then the orange wool scarf my daughter Marsha knitted for me the previous year. On top of that went my North Face winter coat and heavy, water-resistant shoes. I grabbed my ski gloves and keys, locked the door, and pulled on the gloves.

Stepping out of the front door of the building, I pulled up the hood of my coat, covering my head and face except for my eyes, mouth, and nose. I discerned right away that it wouldn't be wise to try to walk in the deep snow of the unplowed sidewalk.

I felt nothing cold at first, as I trudged down the middle of Haviland Street. The air was thick white. Even the black letters forming "Berklee College of Music" down the street were white. When I got to Massachusetts Avenue ("Mass Ave" to Bostonians), the snowplows were out, their huge blades pushing mountains of snow against the curb. A few cars followed the plow. My feet sank three or four inches into the snow. Warm in all my paraphernalia, I felt nothing but a numb nose and the flexing of the muscles in my legs as I pushed and pulled my feet in and out of the snow. Paying no attention to the signal lights, but watching the plows and the cars, I crossed Mass Ave and then Boylston and headed for Newbury Street, fashion alley. The cold air infused me with energy like Southern California weather never had. I could see through the snow for about a block.

On Newbury dozens of men pushed portable snowplows, clearing the sidewalks for the shoppers who would flood the area in a few hours. I had to walk in the street because most of the sidewalks were still deep in snow or occupied by the portable plows. An occasional dog walker appeared like an apparition out of the white. A jogger glided slowly down the middle of the street. Snow hung from the trees like bleached cotton candy. No green showed through on the pines. Bushes looked like a fancy dessert. Everywhere silence pervaded. All sound and even the smells of the city seemed to be absorbed by the snow. A neighborhood that was usually loud with traffic, sirens, horns, and people was as quiet as a cemetery. The motorized plows had not yet come to Newbury. I was hungry, but most of the restaurants didn't open for brunch for another hour, and I didn't feel like usual breakfast fare. I turned up Dartmouth to go over to Boylston, where Legal Seafood might be open for brunch.

Thoughts of a hot bowl of clam chowder made me trudge a little faster, probably too fast for safety on the slick street. My face started to sting, like tiny electric shocks on my skin. The snow had turned to raining ice, but the prickly feeling on my skin brightened my spirits more. I really am perverted, I thought, as a young man lumbered by me, uttering to nobody in particular, "This really sucks." I thought it was glorious.

Boom — a huge block of snow slid off the roof of the nineteenth century public library just behind me. Boylston had been plowed, and traffic crept down the street, so I had to walk on sidewalks that had not yet been shoveled or plowed. My legs were tired and weakened from pushing and pulling through the snow. Nothing was open except Trinity Church and Starbucks.

As I lifted one leg and then the other out of the snow, the Prudential Center and Legal Seafood loomed ahead. It continued to rain ice. My whole face was numb. Time to go in, I thought, and I pushed the revolving door. A blast of warm air hit me in the face. I must admit it felt good to remove all my outer paraphernalia and sit down at the bar at Legal Seafood.

"What would you like to drink?" asked Lacy, the server.

"A glass of Champagne," I said, grinning.

After three years in Boston I moved to Paris, having learned that if I really want to partake of what life has to offer, I mustn't fear change.

BOYD LEMON: After a stellar 40-year career as a nationally recognized attorney, Boyd Lemon discovered his passion, writing, and pursued it in the idyllic coastal town of Ventura, California; the literary, art and music scenes of Boston; a Bohemian year on the Left Bank in Paris; and finally, by the bucolic rivers and forests of St. Marys, Georgia, where he currently lives. Boyd's newest book is *Retirement: A Memoir and Guide.* He has published six other books and is working on his first novel. He has four adult children and four grandchildren. His second passion is travel, and he has visited six of the seven continents. Website: www.boydlemon-writer.com

Janet Simcic

OVERCOMING MY FEAR OF PINK

AUTUMN! IT EVOKES WARM MEMORIES for me of growing up on the East Coast. I recall leaves changing from green to crimson and bright yellow, and delicious air brisk in my nostrils.

My perennial October joy ended abruptly in 1993 when I became that one out of seven women diagnosed with breast cancer. Thanks to the efforts of the Susan G. Komen Foundation and other organizations, October is now breast cancer awareness month, and the color *pink* is prominent on TV commercials, clothing, perfume bottles, sports team gear … you name it. I couldn't appreciate it more. But for the first ten years after my double mastectomy and a year of anguishing chemotherapy, every October brought back fear and pain, and pink reminded me daily of being in survival mode. Pink had come to represent nausea, sleepless nights, baldness, and anxiety about whether I'd live to see grandchildren born, if I'd suffer, when I would have a recurrence.

I turned fifty the year of my diagnosis. It started out fine. Took care of all my doctors' appointments, my yearly mammogram, screeched into menopause, went on estrogen therapy — and then it happened. Two days after my mammogram, I got *the call.*

"Mrs. Simcic, this is Dr. Hopkins' office. We need you to have additional views for your recent mammogram."

I made the appointment, heart hammering, and feared it wasn't good news. I endured the extra scans, had the ultrasound, went home and cried. The next day the call came.

"Mrs. Simcic, there's been a change in your breasts. You need to review your film with a surgeon."

A good friend worked for Dr. Baick, an M.D. who'd recently started a practice just for breast cancer patients ... with his own staff oncologist and plastic surgeon. I made the appointment, picked up the film, and peeked at it in the parking lot. There was the tumor, smaller than the nail on my pinkie finger, exactly like photos of breast cancer in brochures I'd read. It beamed like a shining star.

Tears fell, and I called my husband, Bill. We met with Dr. Baick, who reviewed the film and said, "A lumpectomy should take care of a tumor this small. Here are the orders for a needle biopsy, and your surgery for next Friday."

It's not fun to sit in front of an X-ray machine and have someone place a marker in your breast, followed by a long needle to aspirate tissue. But I forced myself through it by prayer. The lumpectomy surgery was quite simple, with little pain or recovery time. "Got it all," he said. "We'll call you with results next week." He called the next week for a follow-up appointment. That wasn't good news. It meant something bad. Bill and I held each other tightly, prayed some more, asking for that miracle, and drove to the office.

Dr. Baick said, "Bill, I'm going to talk to you because your wife is in shock and may not understand."

But I listened to every word. Not only did I have in situ cancer, making it impossible to have clear margins, but the cancer had already spread to my lymph nodes. It was estrogen receptive. Dr. Baick delivered the verdict. I needed a total mastectomy.

Two weeks later, I sat in the plastic surgeon's office as he tried to convince me that the horror stories of silicone breast implants were exaggerated. He threw one across the room to demonstrate. Being a fearful person, I opted for the saline. Long before Angelina Jolie made headlines, I chose to have the other breast removed as well. Having estrogen-receptive cancer, along with my family history of my dad's prostate cancer and my mother's ovarian cancer, I had serious risk factors.

By the end of the month, I had nice implants (chosen after feeling the implants of many other cancer patients) and started chemotherapy with Dr. Tariq Mahmood, the most compassionate doctor I've ever met.

The country was in recession in 1993, our business was hitting bottom, my daughter was getting married, and my son was entering his second year at Columbia University. I wept. I'd be bald for my daughter's wedding. Would I ever look like me again? When I told people I had breast cancer, everyone immediately looked at my breasts. It was embarrassing.

Then one night, I scratched my head and a handful of hair came out. Did you know it hurts to lose your hair? It's surprisingly painful. By the end of the second round of chemotherapy, every hair on my body had disappeared. I wore a wig, which I'd throw off the minute I walked into my house.

However, here's the positive side. I got through it. I found out how strong my marriage was. I discovered my friends were really there for me. I became a cheerleader for other women facing this insidious disease. I went back to work, seven days a week throughout my chemotherapy. I was energized, motivated. I began to take on projects I'd put off because I felt I was too busy. I researched my family tree. I traveled to Europe. I learned how to speak Italian. I wrote two books and plan to write at least two more. I accepted *pink* as the color winners wear. I began to live life *one day at a time* and learned: "This is the day that the Lord hath made, let us rejoice and be glad in it."

I've always felt grateful for my life. I've been fortunate. But breast cancer taught me how to turn a tragedy into a triumph. Two years ago,

I was diagnosed with lymphoma. It was easier this time. No color for lymphoma. But I knew in my heart if I could survive one of the most difficult kinds of breast cancer, I could survive lymphoma, too.

It's 2013, and I have joy, twelve grandchildren and counting, speak Italian with gusto, write until my fingers tire, travel. I'm always looking to learn something new, wanting my life to count, to be remembered as someone who faced adversity, survived, and lived life to the fullest.

I'm told the lymphoma will probably return, and my breast cancer might come back. But if and when life throws me a lemon, I'll be gutsy and make *pink* lemonade. And when it's my time to die, I have every intention of arriving at the grave in a pretty pink dress and, as Hunter Thompson would put it, "skid[ding] in broadside, thoroughly used up … and loudly proclaiming, 'Wow, what a ride.'" Never stopped living, never gave up, and never stopped trying.

JANET SIMCIC grew up in Boston, New York, and Michigan. After graduate school, she taught gifted high school students, ran a secretarial service and co-owned a large construction business with her husband.

Her first fiction book was published in 2011. *The Man At The Caffe' Farnese* is available on amazon.com and Kindle. In addition, Janet has freelanced for *The Baptist Bulletin, Travel and Leisure,* and the travel section of *The Orange County Register.* Website: www.janetsimcic.com/site/

Marian Longenecker Beaman

GUTSY IN UKRAINE

T HE GUTSIEST PART OF OUR visit to Ukraine in 2011 was that we didn't use the "return" part of our ticket four days into the trip.

Why, you ask, would you want to leave a country with affectionate, artistic people? With gold-domed cathedrals? With an astonishing exchange rate of 8.97 greve / $1.00 U.S.? With "free" lodging at the home of our host, for heaven's sake?

Well, some background to start. At the invitation of our friend Margot, who runs a charity fund in Ukraine, my husband, Cliff, and I have agreed to present 20 performances in the public schools of Kiev as a gesture of goodwill, all work pro bono. Cliff does art and music shows with historical, character-building, and environmental themes. I am asked to give short lessons in English using plastic eggs to teach the names of colors. Like children everywhere, the youngsters are eager to learn but struggle to twist their tongues around combinations of sounds unfamiliar to their native Russian: pink became pinnnngk to them. I also assist students in cleaning sticks of chalk after each multimedia performance and then make the evening meal at Margot's apartment.

We have known Margot, our host and guide, since she was eight years old, when we were newlyweds. We have a quasi sister/daughter relationship with her. Over the years, we have shared meals on her furloughs home to Florida. In Ukraine, she has built close relationships with her staff of six, who help her design curriculum for use in schools and churches. Children she interacts with adore her warmth and creativity. But from the beginning, Margot alternates between approval and hostility for my husband, Cliff, a baffling, unexplainable response from someone who is the beneficiary of free programs along with funds for meals and transportation for her staff as we travel.

Although we came at her invitation, we have to wonder, "Does she consider Cliff a threat for some reason? Is she envious? Something else?" Fortunately, her staff is most gracious, the schoolchildren so very appreciative in Kiev, Zhitomer, and neighboring villages. Standing ovations for Cliff's performances, with requests for autographs. Plus grateful administrators.

And there is a lot to love here culturally: *Zorba, the Greek* ballet at the Kiev Opera House, a magnificent edifice shaped like a fancy cake, and the Moscow Circus performers. Even the Ukraine's paper money is decorative. And art everywhere! Walls of World War II-vintage schools feature cute, flowery cutouts to celebrate spring. Students are all decked out in formal outfits for class: boys in suits, girls in black-and-white outfits, the older girls with stiletto heels (odd by American standards, but attractive nonetheless).

Yes, there are hardships, some anticipated, and some not. At the whim of city fathers, the hot water in Kiev is turned off for days on end. Everywhere we go, the toilets are of the low-down variety: Let's just say I'm glad I practiced my squats in the gym before the trip.

In school restrooms, there rarely is soap, and I carry sections of toilet paper in my fanny pack everywhere we go. There is absolutely *no* toilet paper in any of the school restrooms we visit. In fact, prior to the trip, Cliff's easel and accoutrements, including lecturer's chalk, were all cushioned with dozens of rolls of toilet tissue for us and the staff, packed to sail on a freighter through the Black Sea and shipped into Kiev before our arrival. Once we have to pay 56 kopeks in Sevastopol to use the urinal, but there is toilet paper provided and a woman who mops up!

Beyond the hardships and adjustment to cultural differences, I treasure the new friends I meet: Anya and Sergei, whose hearts are big enough to adopt several children from the bulging orphanages in the city in addition to their own brood. Good-natured Demetri, who translates Cliff's remarks into Russian. Roman, who knows how to talk himself out of a traffic ticket. Then there are Alona and Tanya, who should be awarded gold stars for hospitality. A lovely dinner at the home of Pastor Peter and his wife, Lilly. Petite, unassuming Dr. Olga, M.D. and Ph.D., researcher with mice, who escorts us all around Crimea near the end of our stay, touring the tsar's palace, visiting Yalta, and learning that the Black Sea is actually bright blue!

Miraculously, our trip continued beyond the fourth day to embrace a culture we may never have experienced otherwise and friendships that continue to this day. We get updates from many of these newfound friends. In fact, Roman is one of my friends on Facebook! Lesson learned? Rise above the pettiness and concentrate on the positive — a lesson that, apparently, I needed to relearn.

We fly to Paris on the return trip. At Charles de Gaulle Airport, we go to the transfer desk by tram but find a long queue. When I face the agent, I practice my wobbly French to ask directions to the gate: "Quelle direction est la porte trente-deux?" She replies sweetly, "Prenez l'escalier derrière vous." Okay, it's behind me and up a flight of stairs.

"Magnifique," her smile says. And that's how I remember our trip to Ukraine.

MARIAN LONGENECKER BEAMAN'S life has been characterized by reinvention: Pennsylvania Mennonite girl becomes traveling artist's wife in Florida, then English professor with credits in the Journal of *The Forum on Public Policy* published by the Oxford Round Table. Along with her work as a community activist leading a neighborhood to take on Walmart expansion, she is a writer and blogger in this second phase of her career. Fitness training and Pilates classes at the gym have become a metaphor for her mind-flexing experience as a writer, mining stories from her past along with reflections on current events. www.plainandfancygirl.com

Felicia Johnson

THE BEST KIND OF THERAPY

WHEN I WAS SIX YEARS OLD, my second-grade teacher, Ms. Medley, gave me my first writing assignment. The only rule of the assignment was to write one paragraph about something that I wanted. My assignment was titled: *I Want A Dog*. Paragraph one started with how much I would have liked to have a dog (very much), why (because they are so cute and fluffy), and why I couldn't have one (our home was too small). Then, when I finished with the reason I couldn't have a dog, I began a second paragraph. Then a third and a fourth. By the time I ran out of paper, I had written 100 pages.

Monday morning came, and Ms. Medley read a few students' paragraphs aloud. When she finally got to mine, she held up my notebook to the class and said, "Felicia has written a novel! It is called *I Want A Dog*."

After school, Ms. Medley took the time to explain to me what a novel is. She explained that a novel is a prose narrative made up of characters, emotions, and expressions. She told me that the writers who produce these novels are called authors. Ms. Medley said that if I kept writing, filling up a hundred-plus pages of notebooks, then one day I could be an author.

I asked her if I was in trouble for doing the assignment incorrectly. Ms. Medley's reply was not what I expected. She said, "Felicia, the assignment was completed correctly as long as it was written by you and you feel that everything that you want to express is in the story." I said it was, and she replied, "OK. You're a writer. Keep on writing." I never forgot Ms. Medley's encouraging words, and I kept writing through my adolescent years.

Growing up, I suffered from child abuse. My parents had me when they were very young, and my mother was single for the majority of my teenage years. As the oldest of my mother's four children, I took on a lot of responsibility, taking care of my brothers and sister. Being forced to grow up fast had its consequences.

When I was fifteen years old, I had a best friend named Holly. Holly was diagnosed with borderline personality disorder (BPD). My friend lost her battle with BPD and committed suicide when she was only fifteen years old.

I developed major depression, and I was put on medication and saw a therapist. However, I found that writing was the best therapy. I wrote journals about my memories of Holly and what it was like growing up. Before I realized it, the journal had turned into a memoir of great memories. Coping with depression through writing saved my life.

Years after Holly's death, I had an idea to write a story about a girl who suffered from depression and BPD but survived all she had been through. I started on a story with Holly in mind and combined a bit of what it was like growing up for me and surviving my own experiences.

I knew that if I continued down the path of healing, through my writing I would be able to help others who had suffered from child abuse and mental illness. Therefore, I continued to write and produced my first novel, called *Her*. *Her* is a story of hope and survival.

Speaking out through writing is the gutsiest thing I can say I've done. I use writing to help others who have suffered abuse, and people who struggle with mental illness along with their families, friends, and loved ones. I share my story to help others, instead of using it as an excuse not to accomplish my goals and move forward in life.

I'm a youth advocate, mentor, and behavioral health worker. I speak out against child abuse, and I work to raise awareness about mental illness, particularly personality disorders. As a mentor, I've helped youths who are in patient treatment transition to an independent life outside of the hospital. I've helped them prepare for job interviews, pay their own bills, and apply for college after finishing high school. I've seen many youths who struggle with mental illness transition from being completely dependent on the system to gaining their independence and living on their own.

I'll never forget the first time Ms. Medley told me what an author is. From that moment, I knew it was my calling. Writing is my life because writing saved my life. Writing brings out many relatable emotions and thoughts to share with others. I don't write only for myself; I write for others. I try to always write with a purpose. As Maya Angelou said, "I've learned that people will forget what you said, people will forget what you did, but people will not forget how you made them feel." I write to make my readers feel. Writing about the truth and speaking out is the gutsiest thing I've done and will continue to do.

FELICIA JOHNSON is a writer, mental health worker, student, and big sister. She loves ice cream and seeing her little sister, Laura, smile. She is an active youth mentor at Youth Villages Inner Harbour and article writer for The Personality Disorder Awareness Network (PDAN). Johnson's debut novel, *Her*, is a survivor's tale of endurance that illustrates the complex illness of borderline personality disorder. Her website is: www.herthebook.com

Ian Mathie

THE CAMEL AT NGIOURI WELL

I TRAVELLED SOUTH FROM the Bilma oasis, in the empty wastes of the Sahara, with a small Hausa salt-trading caravan. We had been going five days when we reached the well at Ngiouri. Situated below a small hillock with a stone cairn on top, the well had not been visited by anyone else for some weeks, and we found it choked with windblown sand. It took us twelve hours digging, passing baskets of sand up a human chain to the surface for disposal, before we were able to get at the water, which collected in a small cleft in the bedrock.

By the time we were able to begin watering our camels, I had developed a slight fever but still had to wait for a drink, as the animals are always watered first. The well's refill time was slow, so it took almost half an hour for each of the fifteen camels to drink before any of the humans got a drop. Because I was an outsider who had joined the caravan for my own convenience, my camel and I had to wait until almost the last.

By the time my turn came the fever had developed, and I was confused and fumbling, on the verge of delirium. When my camel had drunk the first of its intended two buckets of water, something spooked it and it shied away, wandering off into the darkness before I could get a firm grip on its lead rope. Everyone else was too preoccupied with making his or her own food and settling down for a good night's sleep to notice. It was eighteen hours after we arrived before I finally got a drink myself, having been without water since the previous morning when our original supply ran out.

When dawn came there was no sign of my camel, and the rest of the caravan was preparing to move on. Their party included old people who were in need of medical attention and could not afford to delay. Hamidi, the caravan master, came to speak to me, to tell me they could not afford to delay. I would have to remain at the well until my camel came back, while the rest of them went on.

"Will it come back?" I asked.

"Oh, certainly," he assured me. "A camel can only go nine days without drinking if it has had a full stomach. Yours had only had one bucket. It will be back before that, as there is no other water within range. Camels can smell water from many miles away." He said the pause would give me time to recover from the fever.

Hamidi also assured me that if anyone else found my camel he would bring it here. A white man travelling alone with a camel does not go unnoticed. I and my camel had aroused plenty of discussion at Bilma. Another caravan was due to follow this route four or five days behind us, so if all else failed I could continue my journey with them.

"Just be patient," he said as he left me, and by noon the caravan had moved on and disappeared over the southern horizon.

Once I was on my own, I moved my camel saddle and baggage panniers onto the rising ground of the cairn-topped hillock. Using a pair of four-foot poles, carried for the purpose, and a cotton sheet, I rigged an awning to provide shade, attaching the back to the saddle and weighting the corners with small stones collected from the desert around me. The shade was welcome in the rising heat, and the slightly elevated position enabled me to see some miles back down the route along which the next caravan from Bilma should come. It had the disadvantage of exposing me to the incessant, grit-laden wind.

Late that afternoon as I dozed, I heard a familiar gurgling noise. I sat upright, expecting to see the second caravan arriving, but the shimmering desert was empty. When the sound came again, I scrambled from my shelter and looked around. Still there was nothing to see. It was only when I staggered farther up the mound, and could look down the other side, that I saw the source of the sound.

A large bull camel was couched, its left foreleg bound with rope to stop it rising. When it saw me, it let out another gurgling bellow. It was completely alone, and there was no sign of anyone camped nearby. I wondered where its owner was and how long it had been there. Had it been there before the caravan left? I had seen nobody else at the well, which was in full view of my awning.

It was quite possible the camel had been there for several days, and it had clearly not had a drink in that time. I lurched back to my awning, pulled out my canvas bucket and a half-filled water skin, and dragged these over to where it sat. Its head came down immediately as I poured water into the bucket, and in seconds it had sucked this dry. I refilled it twice and, as I pulled the bucket clear, the camel shook its head vigorously, its lips flapping and spraying frothy saliva in an arc that glistened in the bright sunlight.

Still not fully recovered from the fever, I lurched back to my shelter and lay down to rest. I awoke in the cool of predawn, feeling thirsty. My water skin was all but empty, so I took it down to the well to refill it.

The wind, which never stops in this part of the desert, had deposited a generous pile of sand in the well, and it took me all morning to dig this out before I could get at the water. Even then it took the cleft a long time to refill each time I had taken a couple of bowls full and decanted it into my water skin. The water was brackish, tasting very like Epsom Salts and I knew not to drink too much in one go or the results could be uncomfortable. It was almost dark by the time I dragged my full water skin out of the well, so I returned to my shelter, ate a few dates, and rested.

For two more days I rested and waited. Each evening, when I climbed the hillock to look, the bull camel was still there, waiting patiently. It gurgled when it saw me, but made no effort to rise. After two days, feeling better myself, I gave it another drink.

On my seventh day at the well, the camel's owner turned up, with two other camels and a small flock of scrawny goats. He watered his animals, thanked me for giving water to the bull, and gave me a gourd of fresh goat's milk. Then he bid me a safe journey, and in minutes he and all his animals had disappeared over the horizon.

I sat, alone, through the heat of the day. Just before sunset my own camel came back. She sucked greedily at the first bucket of water I offered, and then, on a whim, I pulled the bucket aside and refused to give her more. I tucked the lead rope into her head collar and let her go. After a moment's hesitation, she turned and ambled off into the desert as before.

Five days later there was still no sign of the second caravan from Bilma and I was beginning to wonder if I had made a very foolish mistake. As the sun kissed the western horizon, I heard a familiar gurgle. My camel had returned.

This time I watered her well and did not let her go.

IAN MATHIE: Born in Scotland and taken to Africa at age three, Ian Mathie grew up in the bush. After short service as a pilot in the RAF, he returned to West Africa as a rural development officer. Well-adapted to living in the bush, Ian worked with isolated societies, sharing their hardships and understanding cultures from the inside.

Following political changes, he returned to the United Kingdom and retrained as an industrial psychologist. Since then he has designed and run award-winning personnel development programmes in UK, Europe, and Africa.

Now restricted from travelling by a medical condition, he lives in south Warwickshire with his wife and dog, and writes books, mainly about Africa. Website: http://www.ianmathie.com

Jessica O'Gorek

Why I Love Crack Cocaine

"I do not encourage the use of any legal, illegal, or recreational drugs, period. This is a story and not a love confession for crack cocaine. I condone no mind-altering substances, not even alcohol, which is why I haven't even had a beer in over TEN years!"
—Jessica O-Gorek

WHEN I WAS EIGHT YEARS OLD, my parents divorced: strike one. By the time I was ten, my mother was bipolar and had spent a good six months in Western State Mental Hospital: strike two. Then she took off to Richmond, and I didn't see her for a good year. I was told she was sick and couldn't handle raising me at the time: strike three. At twelve, I decided I wanted to smoke cigarettes and, being the all-knowing teenager, I proceeded to replace the love I was lacking from my mother by getting it from boys. So I started having sex and sneaking out in the middle of the night: strike four. At thirteen, I met my future husband: strikes five, six and seven. At sixteen, I got drunk for the first time and spent a good half an hour retching in my boyfriend's front yard: lost count! When I reached seventeen, my father didn't know what to do with my sorry ass anymore, so he left me at his house and went to live thirty minutes away with his girlfriend. At eighteen, I got married, bought a house and two acres in the country, and smoked a joint for the first time: strike infinite!

What follows is a whirlwind story about spousal, drug, and all forms of abuse, combined with motherhood, addiction, recovery, and chasing my ultimate dream of becoming an author.

Now, where was I? Oh, right, eighteen. I quickly learned that my husband and high school sweetheart was a controlling and physically and emotionally abusive redneck, and that the only way we could tolerate each other was by smoking a lot of weed. Twenty: It's time for a baby! Yeah, I thought, maybe a crying, stinky swaddled mess of adorable would save our marriage. Ha! Thankfully, my daughter, combined with a new drug, cocaine, would be the beginning of the end of my first pitiful marriage. When he decided to hit me in front of her when she was ten months old and strangled me because I wouldn't let him put coke on certain body parts, I decided it was time to leave.

At twenty, I took my girl and ran over to my dad. I met up with my other high school sweetheart, got my own place for the first time, and got clean for about six months. Then I met White Boy Larry, the equivalent of my pimp in disguise. White Boy Larry was his code name to get into the crack house where he introduced me to my new lover, Crack.

Crack and I got along splendidly! He would keep me up all night, make me feel like superwoman, helped me lose weight, and cleaned my house, the perfect life companion, right? Our relationship was one of few words and little emotional growth. He always seemed to know what I wanted and when I wanted it, and I couldn't get enough of him! If he was gone, even for a second, I would miss him so badly! I would go out at all odd hours of the night to try and find him and bring him safely home. The only issue was he wanted me all to himself and would rarely give up any space in my brain or heart so I could share it with my daughter.

After six months, our beautiful relationship began to take a serious nosedive. When he found out I was cheating on him with Sam, my soon-to-be second husband, he got a little angry. When I told him my daughter meant more to me than him, he got even angrier; so angry that he kept me up for three days, so stressed out that I developed hives and couldn't eat or drink anything!

Finally, with Sam's encouragement, I was able to break up with Crack. Sam told me I had an addiction to Crack and that I needed some serious help to get over him. At ninety pounds, with hives and an empty shell of a soul, I made a decision to enter into substance abuse counseling with sixteen other addicts like myself.

That was in 2003, when I was 23. I had a few epiphanies while in counseling. As I sat in a room with sixteen other ladies, the counselor told us all that one of us would still be clean within one year's time. As I looked at the other ladies with their scars and tats, the empty sadness in their eyes reminded me of wounded animals in a cage. I decided that I would be that one person and that no one would stop me. For once, my stubbornness was on my side and not against me.

I quit using all legal (alcohol included) and illegal substances. I became a wonderful mother, married Sam in 2005, quit smoking cigarettes in 2007, began to exercise religiously, and became a vegetarian. Today, I have been clean for eleven years, I run three to five miles, four days a week, and I earn a dependable $50K a year. I have a car that's paid for, my own place, and a fabulous 13-year-old girl. I'm a published author, and I just took a huge leap of faith by leaving my second husband because I wasn't in love anymore. My next step at self-preservation is getting off my antidepressants and working my way to the top of a best sellers list!

So I love crack cocaine because it took me to the dungeon so I could appreciate moving up to the tower of the castle. Without starving in that dungeon's shadows, I never would have been able to be thankful for any light that crept through the bars of my cell. It has taught me that if I love myself, everything else will fall where it's meant to. Not always where and when *I* want it to, but where it's *meant* to.

JESSICA O'GOREK: I was born in Chesapeake, Virginia, in 1979. I was raised within the American Indian religion and was taught great respect for the earth and all its living beings. I grew up admiring my father, Barry Weinstock, an author. He took me around the country to different places so he could write his wilderness survival books. When I was twelve, I started writing novels by hand. My first was two thousand pages. In October of 2012, I lost my father to lung cancer. As he lay in his hospital bed, I promised him I would be a famous author one day. He looked at me with all of wisdom and sadness and replied, "Honey, I don't doubt it."

The dedication in my first published book, *Gemini Rising: Ethereal Fury,* reads, "I did, Daddy! I finally did it! This one's for you." Website: www.geminirising1.blogspot.com

Laurie Buchanan

FROM GED TO PH.D.

FOLLOWING THIRTEEN MONTHS behind my only sibling's footsteps was hard. Really hard. From elementary school on, Julie was a glowing student. Barely having to crack a book, she absorbed, digested, and understood information seemingly by osmosis, and had fun doing it.

She maintained straight A's throughout her academic career, was listed on every honor roll, was valedictorian of her graduating class, and earned a scholarship to San Diego State University. I, on the other hand, struggled to maintain a C average and ran away from home at the age of fifteen.

Let's take a moment and rewind…

I thought I was stupid. Compared to my sister, it certainly appeared that way. However, it wasn't until many years later I discovered that I learn in a different way from how I was being taught. There are three learning styles:

Auditory learners grasp things by *hearing* them — the worst test type for them is reading passages and writing answers about them in a timed test. They're best at writing responses to lectures they've heard. They're also good at oral exams.

Visual learners comprehend through *seeing* things — the worst test type for them is listen and respond. They're best at diagramming, reading maps, essays (if they've studied using an outline), and showing a process.

Tactile (kinesthetic) learners understand things through *experiencing/doing* them — the worst test type for them is lengthy tests and essays. They're best at short definitions, fill in the blanks, and multiple choice.

The general teaching population when I was in school were auditory teachers. As a heavily tactile learner, with a smidgen of visual thrown in for good measure, I was missing the boat!

Fast forward...

When you run away from home, you also run away from school. Had I done any advance planning — which I had not — I would have known that if you leave high school before you graduate, you can't test for a General Education Diploma (GED) until two years *after* your graduating class.

"Why not?" I asked. The firm but polite career counselor at Clark College, the local junior college in Vancouver, Washington — a few states away from home — explained that if that particular stopgap measure weren't in place, every high school student would jump ship early.

I had lied about my age and was working at Fred Meyer, a large, everything-under-one-roof store. Over the next few years I worked my way up to managing the women's wear department, then added men's wear, and topped it off with furniture.

During this window of time I was gaining valuable life experience. Part of this seat-of-the-pants wisdom was learning to say, "I don't understand. Can you please explain it differently?" And then I noticed that no matter how many times someone "told" me, it wasn't until they "showed" me that I got it! When shown, I not only met but exceeded what was expected of me.

Managing all of those departments wasn't enough to keep my mind fully occupied. If testing for the GED was out of the question at that time, I wanted to know if they'd at least let me take CLEP tests (College Level Examination Program) so I'd be ready to hit the ground running at the junior college level once I had my diploma in hand. The same polite but firm career counselor I'd spoken with before explained, "That program is for high school graduates and people who've already earned their GED."

I'd left high school as a sophomore in 1973. Four long years I waited and prepared to take the GED examination. On a hot day in late June of 1977, with the cut-grass tang of summer in the air, I slipped into a front-row seat at the testing center, one of about twenty people enveloped in the sterile classroom setting. The examiner explained that talking was expressly prohibited.

The all-day test was given in seven parts: Language arts (writing); 50 questions, 75 minutes. Language arts (reading); 40 questions, 65 minutes. Social studies; 50 questions, 70 minutes. Science; 50 questions, 80 minutes. Math (calculator allowed); 25 questions, 45 minutes. Math (calculator *not* allowed); 25 questions, 45 minutes. U.S. Constitution; 45 questions, 60 minutes.

Head held high with a face-splitting grin, I left the facility with every confidence I'd aced the test. Six weeks later I received my GED certificate in the mail. And that was just the beginning. Over time I earned my associate's degree, then a bachelor's, followed by a master's degree. Finally, two weeks before my fiftieth birthday, I sat and defended my Ph.D. thesis.

Hard-wired for buoyancy and tenacious as a terrier, when I set my mind on something I go after it with tremendous resolve. It took a while, but I eventually went from GED to Ph.D.

You might be wondering why I ran away from home. *Ah, that's another story …*

LAURIE BUCHANAN.

Board certified with the American Association of Drugless Practitioners, Laurie Buchanan is a holistic health practitioner and transformation life coach. With the philosophy of *"Whatever you are not changing, you are choosing,"* Laurie works with the whole person, helping him or her turn intention into action; bridging the gap between where an individual is and where he or she wants to be — body, mind, and spirit. Website: www.tuesdayswithlaurie.com

Jon Magidsohn

MOURNING THE LOSS OF MY WIFE
WITH MY TEN-MONTH-OLD SON

M Y TEN-MONTH-OLD SON, Myles, and I had been on the road
for two weeks by the time we crossed the border from Kansas to
Colorado. We had spent hours driving through blanched wheat fields;
now the landscape suddenly turned green. Rambling stands of cot-
tonwood trees sprouted from the moist woodlands, which drank from
the streams fed by constant mountain runoff. Myles, rear-facing in his
car seat, watched the great plains drifting away into his horizon while,
about eighty miles in front of me, I could see the approaching Sangre
de Cristo mountains fading into view, the red sandstone dotted with
blue-green piñon pines as it arched its way down toward New Mexico.
Having endured nearly a week of featureless views, I welcomed the
sight of the mountains like a long-absent parent. My thoughts, which
had been as arid as the prairies this midsummer, were rejuvenated by
Colorado's verdant vista.

Sue had died less than four months earlier, ten months after her breast cancer diagnosis and nearly a year after we learned she was pregnant with our first child. Impending parenthood and countless visits to doctors of various specialities had inured me against recognizing the signs of normal. After she died, normal simply evaporated. What I did recognize, being a widower now miles from home, was that I didn't just grieve for my wife; I also mourned the loss of the future we were supposed to have had together. My instinct as a single dad told me to kick-start the discovery of my new life by taking it on the road. Myles and I had left Toronto in late July with a car filled like a jar of jelly beans and little in the way of a plan. We were moving forward.

Driving had taken on a new characteristic by the time we reached Colorado. It was no longer simply meditative and cathartic; it had become an inevitability, each leg of the journey fulfilling an insatiable urge to be satisfied. Being in the car with my son was as necessary as breathing. To drive was to be. The silver Rav4 had become a part of our mobile family, an extension of me and Myles that sheltered and guided us and, in return, deserved our love and respect.

We were a threesome again, like the trio Myles, Sue, and I never had the chance to explore. We could have been the exemplar of families. Sue and I might have raised Myles to be the perfect combination of his parents: From me he'd be patient, musical, and lighthearted; from his mother he'd be shrewd, dedicated, and fiery. Even before Sue was diagnosed — before the medical incentives — we never wanted a second child. As a threesome we would be complete.

Maybe it was the endless stretch of grey road winding through America, because even though I'd told myself this excursion was all about forward momentum, it began to feel like I wasn't going anywhere. The one-sided conversations with Myles in the backseat did little to distract me from the empty seat next to me. I'd spent so much time with myself recently, I was beginning to forget what it was like to have a partner.

Loneliness crept up on me like a fiend. I thought I was coping well; I thought I was doing everything right. The reverberating blows of death would eventually dissipate, I assumed, but I didn't think I could endure the loneliness. I understood that so-called 'successful' people can be some of the loneliest; movie stars with trampling entourages at their disposal, the embarrassingly rich, princesses. But I considered myself a success simply because I'd chosen to marry Sue. I didn't have fame, wealth, or royal blood, but I did have intimacy and companionship. When Sue died, she took all the fruits of my success with her.

So this was where the strange contradiction started. Deep down at the bottom of that dark, empty hole that Sue left sat jolly young Myles stretching his little arms out as wide as he could and saying to me in his own wordless way, 'Here I am, Daddy, and I love you. I'll hold your hand when you're feeling lonely, and I'll listen to your secrets, and I'll let you cry on my shoulder, and we can be a family.' And if that hole wasn't in the process of growing persistently larger, he might just have been able to fill it up.

Myles had served as the ever-present counterbalance to the weight of sadness since before he was born. The anticipation of his birth gave Sue and me something to look forward to during the months of cancer management. He'd saved us from the constant burden of fear and doubt.

After Sue died, he kept fulfilling his duty as my protector. The grief was manageable because of Myles, whether we were at home or driving through Middle America. I had to look after him so that he'd still be able to look after me. I needed those moments when he'd wrap his arms around my neck with unquestionable affection, those moments talking to him when he'd smile like a faithful companion. And the moments when he'd look at me with his bright, trusting eyes, and I'd know there was love in my life.

After Colorado we spent ten days driving through the desert before reaching the West Coast. Each region had its own unique effect on my moods and the reflections that accompanied them. By the time we returned home to Toronto, almost two months after we left, we'd covered more than 10,000 miles through twenty-three states and two provinces, four time zones and back, gotten two oil changes and emptied one jumbo box of Cheerios one 'O' at a time. I still had a long way to travel before the worst was behind me, but I was confident that my son and I were headed in the right direction.

JON MAGIDSOHN is originally from Toronto, Canada. He's written about fatherhood for *dadzclub.com, the Good Men Project, Today's Parent,* and *Mummy and Me* magazines. He's also been featured on *Chicago Literati* and the *What's Your Story? Memoir Anthology* (Lifetales) and currently publishes three blogs. He's been an actor, singer, waiter, upholsterer, sales representative, handyman, and writer. He moved to London in 2005, where he received an MA in creative writing (nonfiction) from City University. Jon, his wife, Deborah, and their son, Myles, are now in Bangalore, India, where Jon writes full-time. www.jonmagidsohn.com

Gillian Jackson

WHY DID I CRACK AFTER FORTY YEARS OF SILENCE?

THE COMPLEXITIES OF KEEPING SECRETS can be a heavy weight to carry around; a burden that grows heavier with passing time and, like telling lies, compounds as the secret ages. When I reached the grand old age of fifty, my life began to crumble and my secret came out. As a little girl, I was sexually abused by an 'uncle' over a period of three or four years, abuse that began when I was about four years old.

I cannot claim that my life was completely ruined by this experience. The inbred 'survivor instinct' has given me a degree of strength, and I entered into a happy marriage and gave birth to two wonderful children. I also enjoyed a successful career as the owner and manager of a day nursery in my hometown in North East England.

So why did I crack after over forty years of silence? With hindsight I can identify a number of incidents that perhaps were triggers, bringing old and painful memories to the fore. Working in child care, it was inevitable that at some point I would encounter instances of abuse.

Generally, I could be objective and professional in such cases. But in the later years of my work at the nursery, we cared for a little girl who presented physical signs of sexual abuse. It was an upsetting case, and I floundered somewhat in my responsibilities. I passed the case on to my deputy, which turned out to be the correct thing to do.

But the incident forced me to acknowledge that I had buried trauma from my own childhood, which I had been hiding from myself as well as the rest of the world. I sank into depression, and my usual 'pull yourself together' attitude failed me. This coincided with a medical problem that forced me to retire from my work in the nursery, a career choice that had probably been shaped by my early life experiences. I can also now acknowledge that I had been an overprotective mother. Not to the point of being suffocating, but I trusted no one to care for my own children as well as I could. Fortunately, they have grown into happy, well-adjusted adults of whom I am extremely proud.

Another significant contribution to eventual breakdown was a new role in life as a grandmother. This seems a contradiction, as becoming a grandparent is one of life's best experiences. I found it every bit as emotional as becoming a mother had been twenty-eight years previously. All my maternal feelings were again brought to the fore, coupled with that overwhelming protective instinct that almost knocks you off your feet. It was a wonderful time in many respects, and I had the privilege of attending my first grandchild's birth—amazing. But I felt lost, scared, and fearful of the future.

I am fortunate in having an extremely caring husband who played an enormous part in helping me overcome my negative childhood experiences. He is the one in whom I first confided and who persuaded me to seek help from my GP, the start of confronting my past and moving on with my future. And so began the path of recovery.

It was hard to be honest with my doctor, but I soon learned that this was the only way he could help me. Eventually I was referred to a counsellor, who suggested I would benefit from group sessions. Shock!

Horror! It had taken me forty-something years to get to this point; did she know what she was asking?

The answer to this is yes, and I began a journey that was to change my life, a journey that has been an education. I know and understand myself much better now than I have ever done. I don't like everything I've found out about myself, but I have a greater understanding about why I'm the way I am, and why I do what I do. In short, I'm more at ease with myself than I have ever been.

Enough of the negatives. How can I be so positive and fulfilled today? Well, as part of the healing therapy I decided to try writing, a pleasure that I had never had time to pursue. I scribbled furiously, recording all those painful memories and my shifting emotions, and then took great pleasure in tearing the pages into tiny pieces, a truly cathartic process. I also became fascinated with the theory of counselling and, two years later, returned to college to train as a counsellor. Simultaneously, I embarked upon a writing course, so I had two new passions in which to channel my energy.

It's now eight years since I took that difficult step to disclose my past abuse, and I am a changed person (for the better, I hope)! I use the skills learned in counselling by doing voluntary work for an organization that visits and supports victims of crime, and the writing bug has consumed me! I combined my new passions by writing novels about a therapeutic counsellor, Maggie Sayer. The books particularly appeal to women who seem to connect with the emotional content, and I've been thrilled by some of the positive reviews the books have picked up. The first book is simply titled *The Counsellor* and introduces Maggie and three of her clients. It follows their stories, which generally have positive outcomes (I'm a sucker for a happy ending!). But one novel wasn't enough, and there are now two more in the series, *Maggie's World* and *Pretence*, and I'm currently working on number four. The novels sell mainly as e-books, with paperback copies also available. I now have a new career as a writer: I cannot imagine life without my writing projects, and I am rarely without my laptop or a notebook and pen!

Working through past issues was not an easy task. Although I had some excellent support, it was at times a steep path to climb. But I have no regrets, and I thank God for giving me such a new and fulfilling life.

GILLIAN JACKSON is a passionate writer who lives in North East England with her husband, Derek. When prised away from her laptop and writing projects, she works voluntarily for a charity supporting victims of crime, as well as spends time with her four adult children and eight grandchildren. An interest in psychology and counselling inspires her novels, with all three offering readers the unique opportunity of being a 'fly on the wall' in counselling sessions. Gillian tackles gritty contemporary issues in a sensitive, positive, and non-offensive manner. She is a great believer in happy endings!

Website: www.gillianjackson.co.uk

Eleanor Vincent

THE GREATEST GIFT

I STARED OUT THE WINDOW in the neuroscience ICU waiting room. Below me, stick figures moved across achingly green lawns. They looked like a cardboard tableau of normal life. Mt. Diablo's sawtooth outline cut through a ribbon of clouds. A grandfather of a mountain, its hulking presence loomed above the rolling hills and valleys of Contra Costa County, a collection of suburban towns east of San Francisco. My older daughter Maya's accident had happened three days earlier on a hot April afternoon in the foothills of Mt. Diablo.

She had hiked to a meadow laced with oat grass and wildflowers. A ravine full of scrub oak and laurel trees tumbled down to a dry creek bed. One of her friends dared her to ride bareback on a horse they found there unfenced and unsecured. The animal reared and threw Maya to the ground with such force that she never regained consciousness.

For the last 72 hours, we had endured the hell of waiting at Maya's bedside.

Now, I looked at my watch, steeling myself to face the double doors that led into the intensive care unit and another ten minutes with my comatose child. I lifted the house phone.

"This is Maya's mom. Can I see her now?"

"Yes," a voice answered. "I'll buzz you in."

I walked toward my daughter's bed, past the curtains surrounding families bent over other silent forms. After I had spent three days of willing my daughter to recover, an impossible thought dawned — *Maya might not make it.* When I reached her bedside, I took her hand in mine.

"Sweetheart, it's Mom. I've been telling you that you will get well. But maybe what I want isn't what matters."

A roar filled my brain. I shook my head, trying to silence my own resistance. I spoke to my nineteen-year-old daughter, saying out loud what I would never accept in my heart. "You decide, honey. I won't hold you back."

I looked down at the beautiful young woman she had become. Maya's face, inanimate as ice, was rosy-cheeked, bride-like against the stark white sheets.

I leaned into her and whispered the biggest lie of my life, never doubting she could hear me. "I'll be all right, sweetheart, if you need to go."

I wanted to throw myself across her chest and give in to hours of suppressed weeping. But then I had a new thought: *If I break down, it will be too hard for her to die. My task now is to let her go.*

Maya's chest rose and fell. The ventilator hissed, the monitors beeped, a fiber-optic cable snaked into her skull to measure the pressure inside her brain. Over the last three days I had become expert at reading the peaks and valleys on the monitors.

I whispered, "It's between you and God, now, Maya."

✳ ✳ ✳

The next afternoon, Maya's brain surgeon, Dr. Carr, asked to speak with us about the results of the cerebral blood flow study he had ordered.

One of the nurses gathered us into a windowless conference room where a hospital social worker sat at the opposite end of the conference table, looking grave and sympathetic.

Dr. Carr came in, his white coat flapping, and sat down at the head of the table. I sat on his left side, staring at him.

"The test we did shows how much blood is flowing to the brain." He spoke to the wall, not looking at us. "There is none, absolutely none; zero blood flow. I've declared her brain dead."

I could not move, or even blink. A collective gasp filled the cramped room. Maya's boyfriend, Dale, groaned. My ex-husband, Dan, put his head in his hands.

"I've called in a second surgeon to confirm the diagnosis of death by neurological criteria," Dr. Carr said. He spoke with exaggerated calm, seemingly oblivious to the emotions swirling around him.

My eleven-year-old daughter Meghan leaned against her father and wept. Dale's mother began screaming "No!" over and over.

Hot tears of disbelief trickled down my cheeks. Of all the people in the room, I was the only one who did not move or cry out. I felt granite-hard, yet sensitive as a tuning fork, paralyzed with grief.

For the first time since he had entered the room, Dr. Carr met my gaze. His eyes were like icy blue marbles. "Would you consider organ donation?"

The question hung in the air for a long moment. I pictured families in other hospital conference rooms waiting for bad news.

"Yes," I heard myself say.

Dr. Carr nodded. "At least it won't be a total waste," he said. I recoiled.

He waved his hand in the direction of the ICU and all the high-tech gadgetry keeping Maya's heart beating, her lungs pumping, her blood circulating. I could see he meant that all the effort and resources spent on a hopeless case would not be in vain. But my "yes" meant that the love and energy I had poured into my daughter, her very life, must continue. I could no more accept that Maya was truly dead than I could fly to the moon or allow any vital part of her that could save another human being to go to her grave.

I trembled uncontrollably. I was about to give my daughter away in pieces. *If I had fought harder, could I have held her here?* I gave Maya ultimate freedom, and she took it.

Maya's organs were donated to critically ill patients. My decision saved four lives. Her bone and tissue helped restore sight and mobility to dozens more. In the 21 years since that April day when I made the most difficult decision of my life, I have often wondered what gave me the strength to say yes. From someplace deep within came a sure knowing that donation was the right thing to do. It was the gutsiest moment of my life.

ELEANOR VINCENT is an award-winning writer whose memoir, *Swimming with Maya: A Mother's Story,* was nominated for the Independent Publisher Book Award and was reissued by Dream of Things press early in 2013. She writes about love, loss, and grief recovery with a special focus on the challenges and joys of raising children and letting them go. She is a national spokesperson on grief recovery and organ donation, appearing on radio and television programs across the country. Website: www.eleanorvincent.com.

Shirley Hershey Showalter

STARING DEATH IN THE FACE

Behind all our fears, often hidden even to ourselves, lies one big fear.

Yes, you've got it. The fear of death.

We can't become truly gutsy or courageous until we accept the reality of death, and consciously seek to live deeply and fully in its presence.

I first stared death in the face at the age of six.

It happened this way:

On the evening of Dec. 20, 1954, my younger brother Henry and I were playing in a little stack of hay in our barn, making tunnels out of bales and talking about what we hoped for in our Christmas stockings. Cows chewed contentedly next to us. The DeLaval milkers sounded almost like heartbeats — lub-dub, lub-dub, lub-dub — as they extracted warm milk from each udder.

And then we heard it: a horrible, penetrating, animal-like scream, piercing that night and my life to this day. The terrible sound grew louder as Mother came toward the barn. She ran to Daddy and, still screaming, started pounding him on his chest.

"My baby is dead. Our baby is dead. My baby is dead." That was all she could say. Then she would throw back her head and wail.

I learned a lesson that night that I would have to learn again when my father died at age 55 and when several close friends died in sudden, untimely ways.

We all die.

From then on, life became even more precious. I decided to live twice, once for myself and once for the little sister who lived only 39 days.

When I played softball on the playground, I swung for the fences.

When I read books, like *Little Women,* I identified with the gutsiest character, Jo.

When I discovered you have to go to college in order to be a teacher, I decided to go, even though my parents weren't enthusiastic about the idea. Even though no one else in my family had ever gone.

When I stood up to the bishop in my Mennonite Church and told him that he wasn't practicing what he preached, I stayed true to my convictions.

What does it mean to live twice? How did it change my life?

My childhood and adolescence were never the same after I heard my mother scream and after I touched the cold, white skin of my baby sister inside that sad little casket in 1954.

Death made a searcher out of me. I sought out writers who understood urgency, such as Annie Dillard, who advised:

> "Write as if you were dying. At the same time, assume you write for an audience consisting solely of terminal patients. That is, after all, the case. What would you begin writing if you knew you would die soon? What could you say to a dying person that would not enrage by its triviality?"

I love these words. I try to keep them in mind as I write my stories. But I have to keep something else in mind also.

I believe that death is not the end of life. The writers I love best don't dwell on morbidity. They face death and fear and, while doing so, come home to themselves by coming home to love. Engraved inside their hearts is the reminder that love is eternal.

But it wasn't a writer who taught me that lesson first; it was my mother. After she shook my six-year-old world with her screams and tears, she took solace in her faith and accepted the comfort of friends and family. Depression tempted her. She could have withdrawn from life and hence from her living children. Had that happened, you would not be reading these words.

Sometimes the gutsiest thing we do is to keep on putting one foot in front of another and continuing to live, determined to turn darkness into light.

Next month my mother turns eighty-seven. I no longer fear death because love has triumphed. Whatever is gutsy in me goes all the way back to 1954 and to the woman who never gave up on life, my mother.

SHIRLEY HERSHEY SHOWALTER, author of *Blush: A Mennonite Girl Meets a Glittering World*, grew up on a Lancaster County, Pennsylvania, dairy farm and went on to become a professor and then college president and foundation executive. Find her at her website: www.shirleyshowalter.com

Susie Mitchell

PREGNANCY TO PODIUM

I AM SUSIE, 37-YEAR-OLD FIRST-TIME MOM to a lovely, vibrant baby girl, Tori. I have always had an active lifestyle and loved sports from a young age. Yearning to be really good at something, in fact anything, I had tried everything from shot put to surfing, without much success.

All that changed in the summer of 2011, when I tried track cycling for the first time. Track cycling is carried out at high speeds on an oval, banked track using a fixed-wheel bike with no brakes. It was exciting, and I was hooked immediately. What's more, I was good at it. Racing on the track appealed to my competitive nature, and I clearly had potential, given that I was winning races within a few weeks of getting up on the bike.

When my coach suggested to me that I was good enough to compete in the World Masters Track Cycling Championships in Manchester the following October, a dream was ignited, and it became my focus. I had never competed internationally in any sport and was giddy at the thought of it. Then a massive curveball came my way — I became pregnant.

I did not want to let go of my newfound passion after waiting all these years to find it. I knew so many people who gave up their exercise and hobbies when they became pregnant, and never went back. I wanted to hang onto my sport and my identity through pregnancy and becoming a mum for the first time.

Despite all opinions to the contrary, I was determined to find a way to train safely and effectively through my pregnancy. I had always believed in the benefits of exercise during pregnancy and, being a veterinarian, I had always marvelled how animals took all this in their stride.

I searched the Internet for all I could find on exercise and pregnancy, and found only conservative advice. "Gentle jogging or easy swimming" didn't appeal to me and wasn't going to help me to the World Masters the following October. Turning my back on the Internet and the colloquial advice that abounded, I decided to use science as my guide. Surprisingly, after extensive review of research and scientific papers, I discovered very little evidence to stop me doing pretty much anything while carrying a baby. Through this research and with the help of my coach, I found a way to maintain fitness and train through pregnancy safely.

The best advice I got was from a scientist — who simply said, "Listen to your body". I used this as my mantra when working out. If it felt OK, I did it. I got some funny looks from people in the gym when I was lifting weights and doing core work. I got disapproving glances when I was in the park riding my bike. However, I forged ahead, as my coach and I had devised a set of guidelines for safe cycling that I trusted, giving me the confidence to go on. I worked on things like mental preparation and leg speed when I couldn't do anything else. With some careful planning and research, I found something suitable to do at every stage of the pregnancy. I trained right up until I was 10 days overdue and thought I had it all sorted.

A surprise was in store. You can prepare, but nothing prepares you for it. The impact on your life of having a baby is colossal. My goal had been to arrive at the birth of my baby in peak physical condition. I had achieved this and was probably fitter then I ever had been. I had trained with my bump in ways I had never thought possible, and I had enjoyed every minute of it.

However, when my beautiful, healthy baby arrived into the world, everything went out the window. I had a dose of reality to deal with, grappling with the concept of being responsible for another human being for the rest of my life. I watched through my window as people cycled past while I sat inside in my pyjamas trying to feed my baby and wondering if I would ever get out and ride my bike again. I was physically exhausted from lack of sleep but, more importantly, I was mentally falling apart. I started to wonder if I was ever going to feel normal or be as happy and carefree as before. The whole experience, to my utter shock, had totally floored me.

Salvation came from the bike. Two weeks after the birth I tentatively got back in the saddle and started rolling around. Those first few laps pushing the pedals with the wind in my face felt like pure heaven. I was myself again, doing something for me, but with the bonus of a beautiful baby to go back to after a training session. The effects of sleep deprivation were nearly completely negated by exercise. I hadn't foreseen it, but my sport kept me mentally strong during those difficult first few weeks post-partum, helping me cope.

My return to form came so much quicker than I could have expected: I won my first-ever national medal just six weeks after the birth. I added others in the following months as I went from strength to strength, culminating in the fulfillment of my dream as I travelled to compete in the World Masters in Manchester just four months after Tori arrived.

The event I was targeting was the individual pursuit. I was nervous with anticipation, but when the starting gun went off I knuckled down and rode my heart out, going faster than ever before, scooping the world title by just half a second. A lifelong dream had been fulfilled; I had excelled and was now a world champion!

As I stood on the podium, wearing the rainbow jersey, the gold medal hanging around my neck and the Irish national anthem playing, tears streamed down my face. I knew that none of this would have been possible without having my baby: She trained with me; she gave me energy, inspiration, and focus, and made me strong. By being determined to maintain my identity, I ended up finding a new one, reinventing myself as a credible athlete, discovering it was possible to fuse motherhood and sport at a high level. If I hadn't lived this story, I never would have thought it possible to have both in such perfect synergy.

SUSIE MITCHELL is a 37-year-old first-time mom to a lovely baby girl, Tori. She currently lives in Dublin, Ireland, with her supportive and long-suffering husband, Cormac. Working as a fish vet, she travels the length and breadth of the country visiting fish farms, jumping on and off trawlers in all kinds of weather. Susie has always enjoyed sports, coming from a background of surfing and adventure racing and, more recently, track cycling. She juggles being a mum and a wife, and training and working with reasonable success. Website: www.pregnancytopodium.com

Leanne Dyck

RISING ABOVE EXPECTATIONS

A SOCIAL WORKER TOLD MY PARENTS that they'd have to take care of me for the rest of my life. My principal told them I was uneducable. Thankfully, a resource teacher stepped in on my behalf. She taught me that learning was fun.

The commonly held definition of dyslexia is that it is a difficulty with learning to read. But this is a condensed definition. The challenges people with dyslexia face and the severity of these challenges vary from person to person.

For me, deciphering the social codes has always been a challenge — I never received my copy of that handbook. When I manage to figure out how to respond, often it's too late or, in a rush to be on time, I produce a jumble of poorly pronounced words. Writing allows me to slow down and think. It gives me an opportunity to select the right word, tone, and tense, and to check for clarity and accuracy.

At a young age I learnt that even though my tongue may fail me, my pen seldom will. My first publishing success came when I was still in elementary school — one of my poems was published in the school newspaper. I repeated grade two; but once in middle school, I was determined to excel. So I divorced myself from any social interaction, and books and studying became my world. A middle school language arts teacher introduced me to John Steinbeck, and I fell in love with his writing. Mr. Steinbeck gave voice to the voiceless. Writing gave me a voice. I had lots to say but needed a venue. Through my writing I began to feel heard. I graduated from high school with an award in language arts.

After graduation, the question of what I would do next paralyzed me. I thought living the rest of my life on my parents' sofa was a solution. However, my parents wanted more for me. From early childhood, despite what they'd been told, my parents continued to believe in the soundness of my intellect. Responding to my dad's not-so-gentle pushing, I decided to join Katimavik — a government-run youth group. You'd think that living communally for nine months wouldn't be the best situation for someone with limited social skills. But you'd be wrong. Katimavik was one of the most important experiences in my life. I completed the program and won newfound confidence. With that confidence, I entered university. And I was amazed to find that I was able to obtain and maintain a decent grade point average. I graduated from the program and gained employment as an early childhood educator.

Throughout my life I've been able to play the "help me" card. But in my late twenties I met a man who refused to play the game. That man became my husband, and his special brand of tough love continues to be one of the driving forces behind my success.

Becoming an author had been a dream I'd hidden away since my teens. Weakened by a family tragedy, I shared my dream with my husband. I thought he was going to laugh — but not him. "So, what are you going to do about it?" he challenged me.

The choice was clear: either act to fulfill my dream, or abandon it. From 2006 to 2009, I self-published an audio book, paperbacks, and e-books. Buoyed by these successes, I decided to pursue traditional publishing. So I made a pact to submit one story — of whatever size — every month until something happened. Well, things did start to happen. Within the last five years I've had short stories published in *Island Writer, Kaleidoscope, Canadian Stories, Icelandic Connection,* and *Island Gal.* I've also completed five book-length manuscripts.

But years of self-doubt and low self-esteem have taken their toll, leading to stress-related health problems. I thought joining a peer support group would help. But when I was unable to find a group, I became my own advocate. I now practice tai chi and yoga as well as take Bach flower oil to cope with anxiety.

I'm enheartened by the support now available for children with learning disabilities. At the same time, I am disappointed by the lack of support for adults with learning disabilities. Simply because we manage to jump through academic hoops and graduate doesn't mean our problems disappear. We still face them — every day. Lack of support leaves learning-disabled adults with health and employment problems — some of us wind up on the street or in jail. Potential lost. Lives wasted. But it doesn't have to be this way. Something must be done. All of us deserve an opportunity to create our own success story.

Increasing society's knowledge of dyslexia is a good starting point. And through non-fiction books such as *The Gift of Dyslexia* by Ronald D. Davis and *Understanding Dyslexia and Other Learning Disabilities* by Linda Siegel, this goal is slowly being met. Hoping to help obtain this goal, I've written a novel about my own experiences with dyslexia. And I continue to push myself out of my comfort zone by, for example, reading my writing during open mic nights.

I conclude with a poem:

> I need you to know that I am capable — even when I show my inability.

> I need you to have faith that I will be able to pick myself up when I fall.

I need you to let me show you what I'm capable of — before you help me.

I need you to shout at the top of your lungs, "Yes, you can! If not now — someday; if not without me — with me."

I need you to believe in me, even when — especially when — I don't.

LEANNE DYCK is a women's fiction author. Her stories are about outsiders facing challenges. Within the last five years, her writing has been published in *Island Writer, Kaleidoscope, Canadian Stories, Icelandic Connection,* and *Island Gals* magazines. Leanne has written a fictionalized account of her own experiences with dyslexia. She's seeking a publisher for books one and two in this series. She is currently writing book three. To learn more about this series and to follow her author journey, please visit her blog: http://sweatercursed.blogspot.ca

Victoria Noe

I'm Not Gutsy, But You Are

My Gutsy Story?
I don't have one.

I still think of myself as the painfully shy, often sick little girl who escaped into books. My best friends from high school will tell you I'm famous for "punting." This involved talking myself out of things I really wanted (often involving men).

"Who do you think you are?" was an oft-heard refrain when I was young. I was told by adults other than my parents that I had no right to go to private school. I had no right to go away to college. I had no right to move away from home.

It would've been easy, I suppose, to say, "You're right" and lower my expectations. I didn't, though I was seriously tempted at times. My parents pushed us to succeed, and I didn't want to disappoint them, no matter how much that scared me. At some point I knew I had to give it my best shot, even if I failed. That doesn't mean there weren't nights I cried myself to sleep, wondering if I'd made a decision that would ruin my life.

I realize now that I gave up my initial dream — working in the theater in New York — too soon. I was on track, building a network and experience in Chicago. But I let an emotional trauma sidetrack me and my self-confidence. I still worked in the community for a few more years, but the dream was set aside, a dream I'd had since high school.

Many years later, I believe that everything in your past brings you to where you are now. By my own count, I'm on my fourth career. Writing was something I always enjoyed for my own pleasure, but nothing I ever considered doing professionally.

I was good at all of my careers. I was a damn good stage manager and a decent director. I raised millions when I was a fundraiser for arts, AIDS, and social service organizations, and won national awards when I sold children's books. But writing … this is different.

Writing is terrifying. It's my name on the cover or byline. I write about myself, not just other people. And that scared the hell out of me. That shy girl was back: the one who didn't like people looking at her as she walked down the aisle at her wedding.

I resisted sharing very much of myself for the first year of my blog. I saw myself as more of a teacher than a friend sharing stories. Changing required a good amount of surrender on my part, and a willingness to put myself on the line in a very public way. But if I was to grow, to succeed, I had no choice.

For most of my life, during the course of a conversation, I'd recount something I'd done, and the other person would insist, "Oh, I could never do that." They weren't being judgmental about my actions. They meant they could never see themselves doing what I did.

I always had the same reaction: "Why not?" My accomplishments never felt terribly monumental. Were those things gutsy? They don't feel gutsy to me:

> I've traveled all over the country — and to London —
> alone. Planes, trains, and automobiles have taken me places
> I dreamed of visiting for experiences I'll always remember.

I've moved away from home, without a job or a permanent place to live, to a big city where I knew only two people.

I've approached strangers — famous or not — with requests: donations, autographs, interviews. Long ago I developed a mantra: What's the worst they can do? They'll say yes, no, or maybe. I can deal with all of those possibilities.

Gutsy? No, no, no. Part of my job or an item on my bucket list, but no, not gutsy. Gutsy is for other people.

They're the ones who do spectacular, public things: walking a tightrope across Niagara Falls, going to war, or performing in front of thousands of people. All right, I did do that last one, but it doesn't count: I was so near-sighted I couldn't see past the orchestra pit.

If it's true most people live lives of "quiet desperation," it's also true that they live lives of "quiet gutsiness." Some days, just getting out of bed and putting one foot in front of the other is the gutsiest thing you can do. Maybe a spouse has died, a job has been lost, a mountain of medical bills is piling up. Someone's life has taken a turn, and not for the better. "I don't have a choice," I've heard people say (and said to myself on occasion). "I just have to keep going."

Gutsiness is a choice. It might be a conscious one, with a specific goal, like changing careers. It might be unconscious: a simple acknowledgement that sometimes you just have to keep trying your best to get through it all, in the hope that something better awaits you. I don't think we give ourselves enough credit for that.

My father used to tell my mother that he could throw me into a tiger pit, and I'd be OK: I'd come out bloodied, but I'd make it. I'm pretty sure he didn't mean it literally, though for a long time I didn't understand it. I wasn't even sure it was a compliment.

But last year, at the age of 60, I walked into my first ACT UP (AIDS Coalition To Unleash Power) meeting in New York. Does that mean I'm ready to get arrested for demonstrating? I guess it does. I'm definitely ready to be more vocal about the things that matter the most to me.

There was a moment, early in the AIDS epidemic, when I made a conscious decision to get involved, because I knew I could help. I remember thinking to myself that I did not want to look back and regret not doing anything.

Maybe that's what it means to be gutsy: to choose to live your life without regrets.

Does that make me gutsy? No. I'm doing what I have to do, just like all of you.

VICTORIA NOE has been a writer most of her life, but didn't admit it until 2009. She worked in Chicago's theater community, and then transferred her skills to being a fundraiser for arts, educational, and AIDS organizations. A concussion ended her career as an award-winning sales consultant of children's books, so she decided to keep a promise to a dying friend to write a book, which became the "Friend Grief" series.

Her articles have appeared on grief and writing blogs as well as in *Windy City Times, Chicago Tribune,* and *Huffington Post.* She reviews books on BroadwayWorld.com. Victoria's website is www.friendgrief.com.

Mariana Williams

GUTSY GIRL POWER

I GOT OFF THE PLANE feeling nervous. Having sat in the last row, it took me a while to get out. The pilot was walking way ahead of me when I noticed a text on my phone. "Where are you?"

I sighed and slowed down. Maybe contacting someone through a private detective after a forty-year gap wasn't such a good idea. Was Danelle impatiently tapping her foot at baggage claim? Was she eager to return to her life after meeting me? And, what *is* that life? Aghhh, maybe the text simply indicated she had not recognized me walking past.

I'd been a writer for ten years now, and after penning three novels, my colorful life of peaks and valleys became the focus of my memoirs. The boldest early memories took place with the girl I met at summer camp. We were fifth graders and rode horses, swam, sang, and built a language of laughter that I was betting would be worth the 2,627-mile sojourn across the Pacific Ocean.

Danelle was the friend who always pushed the limits of what was allowed. Now, decades later, I suspected my gutsy friend would either be serving a prison sentence or heading Wall Street. She hadn't shown up for any reunions, and no one had heard a word after high school. My mild obsession about the outcome of her life had me searching the Internet and even looking for her in a crowd. Danelle was my daring alter ego.

Ages twelve through seventeen it wasn't sex, drugs, and alcohol that engaged us — we were just merry pranksters exploring the limits of travel without a car. Armed with imagination and our thumbs, we escaped the hot San Fernando Valley, often hopping off a bus in a random city. Danger was always around the corner, and we saw its shadow. But I trusted my street-smart friend and, aside from us getting picked up by the police as runaways, all was bitchin'.

After a few capers we were restricted from hanging out. Oh, sure. That always works. Ask Romeo and Juliet. The last warning to stay away from Danelle was delivered in my mother's low, guttural growl — at 3 a.m., walking me out of a police station. Danelle and I had feebly explained that we were vacationing at the Beverly Hilton Hotel that weekend. "What's your room number?" barked the policewoman.

"Well, we don't have a room *exactly*," I stammered. "Our stuff is behind a big ol' stack of chairs in the banquet room. We hang out at the pool in the daytime and crash behind the chairs at night. Really, nobody even cares."

My husband's golf buddy was a private eye. It was a gutsy move, but I hired him. It took him about ten days — longer than he predicted. After a few phone conversations, I made plans to fly to Kauai — before one of us died or my fascination lost momentum. Curiosity led to sentimentality and now just the sweaty palms of embarrassment as the twelve-year-old in me looked for my friend's brown, curly mop-head somewhere by the baggage carrousel.

I caught the familiar eyes and serene smile immediately as I came through the door. She was dressed in a feminine, white hippie blouse, jeans, and a sporty hat; something straight out of my closet. My first thought was to wish I had coincidentally worn that same outfit — it would have been a funnier moment. But it wasn't about being funny. We hugged and surprised ourselves, I think, by holding the wordless embrace for a long while. A few tears flowed, and I can't say why. We had not gone through a war together, and neither of us had donated a kidney to keep the other alive. However, Danelle and Mariana were, pound for pound, the best combination of laughs and adventure I'd known. Was there still room for *more* adolescent merriment?

A few years after leaving high school, Danelle dropped out of the mainland's fast lane and opted for the gentle lifestyle of the tropics. She found her niche on the Garden Isle of Kauai and stayed after a brief stint at the hippie colony, Taylor Ranch. She married a local surfer and has two beautiful daughters and three grand girls. With animals in the yard and shells on the windowsill, their life is an endless summer and their home as comfy as a hammock swinging between two palms.

Once inside her house she tossed me a few floral sundresses from her closet to replace my "haole" wardrobe of black and white. Then we did what we do best, hit the road. As we tore around the island in her car, she seemed like a "Guidess," half guide/half goddess — leading us into new adventures. We caught up on decades while we bobbed in the surf of hidden beaches and picnicked on cliffs.

We discovered that we are both happily married; each with two children about the same age, one easier than the other. We cracked up knowing the more difficult child was the most like ourselves. Another coincidence — world travelers, we each had collections of rocks and crystals from foreign lands.

The week passed quickly, as we nibbled shaved ice by day and spent nights under the Hawaiian moon whispering personal stories of unexplainable mysteries, coincidences, and magic moments. Instead of the Beatles, we tuned into the island music. It wasn't Don Ho. It was the beat of waves crashing, the harmony of porch chimes tinkling and — always — girls laughing.

It was a gutsy move to put my ego in my back pocket and bet on girl power, and a friendship that could span years and miles.

MARIANA WILLIAMS is the author of the Veronica Bennett series of romance, comedy, and accidental crime: *Happy New Year, Darling, The Valentine State,* and *Stars or Stripes 4th of July,* which won a 2011 Indie Excellence Book Award. Her book of memoirs will be out in 2014. Mariana was a Moth Grand Slam finalist in the acclaimed storytelling competition held in Los Angeles. She is the Producer of *Long Beach Searches for the Greatest Storyteller,* an event in its fourth season in Long Beach, California. She lives in Southern California with her husband, Oscar-winning songwriter Paul Williams. Website: www.Marianawilliams.net

Yelena Parker

NEXT EXPAT STOP: TANZANIA

HAVE YOU EVER SHARED your story with new and somewhat eager listeners and gotten the reaction, "Wow, that was such a brave thing to do!"? Last year I started feeling as if anything I had done that was remotely brave was in the far-too-distant past. I wouldn't quite call it a midlife crisis; it was more of a realization that something had changed. Then, in a serendipitous moment, there was a tweet in my timeline: "When was the last time you did something for the first time?" Indeed.

My "gutsy" story began almost exactly 15 years ago when I left Ukraine with $600 in my wallet and a one-way plane ticket to study for a master's in business administration in California. On my first international flight to Amsterdam, before connecting to San Francisco, I sat next to one of those American men who came to Ukraine in search of a fiancée. We talked about his desire to find love in an obscure small town where women have no prospects and my dream to see the world on my own. This was before I knew that flight etiquette strongly advises against engaging in annoyingly long conversations with people whom you are stranded with. I was chatty, naïve, and ready to take on the world. What I didn't consider at that time was that it was a gutsy move. When you have nothing to lose, an opportunity to come to the U.S. on a scholarship to work and study, with a chance to make your American dream come true, is really a "no brainer" — at least, that was how I saw it.

Fast forward, and my dream has become more global than I ever could have imagined. Getting an MBA in Silicon Valley during the dot. com crash was far from perfect timing. While we were learning about innovation and planning for rapidly and ambitiously building our big, international careers, the economic climate changed dramatically. One day my fellow students and I had visions of choosing any cool company we wanted. The next thing I knew, I was the lowest-possible-status sales rep, generating leads by walking door-to-door to sell copiers in the spookily empty tech parks along U.S. Highway 101.

Having gotten over the disappointment that many overeducated and underemployed MBAs experience, I fell into a sales operations career in high tech, pretty much starting at the very bottom. In retrospect, it was the best move I could have made. It gave me a chance to see the world and led to opportunities to work and live as an expat in Switzerland and the United Kingdom.

I didn't consider any of these moves as brave at the time. Once you are on a serial expat path, new relocations get easier. You already had to adjust once or twice to a new environment, pick up the pieces of friendships left behind, introduce yourself to new people, and learn or improve a foreign language. You are a chameleon, an international wanderer, and a global citizen. Surely you can do it again!

Last year I looked at a career map that my accidental mentor put together with me six years earlier over coffee. Senior manager responsibilities, check; director level, check; expat assignment, check; executive education program at Oxford University, check; vice president role at a smaller tech company, check. All done. Three years ahead of schedule. What's next? I have finally uncovered that it takes more guts to change direction and do something completely out of character when you have something to lose.

I quit my job and focused on writing a book about expat and life abroad success. Over the last year I kept comparing experiences of my friends — women expats who made their own moves without fear. And there it was, *Moving Without Shaking*. At the same time, I started reevaluating what the meaning of work was for me. Should I join the movement of solopreneurs? Should I go volunteer while I am thinking about what to do next? What do I really know a lot about, besides running sales operations in tech and going to school abroad? I looked for what I had become truly passionate about in my 15 years of corporate adventures and living abroad.

I wanted to do something again for the first time, but it had to be not for my career. March 1 I am starting on a volunteering journey in Tanzania. I have signed up with African Impact, a wonderful organization placing many volunteers in programs all over Africa. The first community project is based in Moshi, on the foothills of Kilimanjaro, and focuses on empowerment of women and children. The second project is for a community in Zanzibar, teaching English and helping the local school. The local communities are in need of educational resources that we often take for granted. My first career was teaching English at a university level in Ukraine. This is an opportunity to take everything I was good at before I started my journey abroad, add in the business experience, and give back in the form of time and knowledge. I was able to move abroad because I met an American professor volunteering in Ukraine, willing to help me with a scholarship. It is my turn to see if I can help someone in one of the countries that my academic mentor is passionate about. I am excited about the learning opportunity, the chance to make a real impact on people's lives, the challenge — and the longest break from paid work I have ever had.

YELENA PARKER is a founder of the expat and executive coaching consultancy Moving Without Shaking Ltd. She is a serial expat, living in the UK — her fourth home country — as of this writing. She blogs about expat and life abroad success at www.movingwithoutshaking.com

Rosalie Marsh

PUSHING BACK THE BOUNDARIES

WHEN INVITED TO SUBMIT my gutsy story, I pondered where to start. Being no spring chicken, I have faced many challenges in my life; but the catalyst in changing me was having hearing aids fitted. (This is not something I normally talk about but, being retired, it doesn't matter anymore — as long as I can hide them.)

Following a traditional route of school, a nice job in an office (bank), marriage, children, and being a stay-at-home mum forever, I eventually went against the fulfilling years of the latter to work in a sales environment — where I *found* myself. After I had a good level of hearing restored, I felt confident about applying for promotion. Previously, I could not fully take part in meetings without saying "pardon?" or "what was that?" as I strove to keep pace. Now, at one such meeting, opportunities to undertake management qualifications were offered. I jumped at the chance and, in complete ignorance, eagerly awaited the programme details. I found that this team-building course involved some very hands-on outward-bound activities at a sea and surf centre on the Isle of Anglesey on the North Wales Coast (UK) over two visits. Suffice to say that I am not an outdoor person!

The course was stretching, to say the least, and pushed me to terrifying limits of endurance as I took part in all sorts of cold and wet activities — abseiling (rappelling), raft making, trekking, putting out to sea on a landing craft, boarding a yacht in the Irish Sea and, horror of horrors, making a sea level traverse. Twenty years later, I can still relive the horror and sheer terror of what I call "rock-climbing sideways with the safety of land above and the depths of the pounding sea below." Stepping off the rock to cross a rocky inlet with only a rope to hang onto really was the moment of truth. You had to have complete confidence that the person at the other side would catch you after you let go of the rock to which you were clinging with fingertips and toes. My confidence increased. Doors of my mind opened and I thought, "I can do this".

However stretching this experience was, it proved to be merely the grounding for what came later as my husband and I became born-again bikers. By now, I had left sales management to work in a further education college (continuing education), taking learning out into the workplace. At the same time, I, too, was studying, undertaking a variety of work-related courses and eventually an education degree.

I had unfulfilled dreams and longed to travel. My husband was not keen on touring in a car on the 'wrong side of the road'. In the midst of my studies and assignments, and our families and grandchildren, he declared that he was hankering after a motorbike following many years of being bike-less. He had nothing with which to tinker! Eventually, the little scooter he pleaded for became a larger one, then a big bike. We had found our lost youth! The world was our oyster! The deal I proposed: If we had a bike, would [he] tour? Could we explore the countries in Europe over which we had flown? Then by chance — serendipity? — I saw a huge, shiny, black beast of a bike in a motorcycle store in North Wales. It was a Honda Gold Wing touring motorbike. Really, a motorised horse if you think about it — at least, that is how the Andorrans ride them.

"This is what we need if we are going to travel," I declared. My husband thought he had died and gone to heaven. A biker's dreams do not normally come true so easily. He turned and walked out before coming back to me.

"But look at the luggage space!" I went on.

"You had better sign up, then."

Our lives changed forever as I sacrificed well-groomed hair and high heels for a crash helmet and biker boots. I was no longer 'Miss Prim and Proper' as my professional colleagues' perceptions of me changed.

I was forty-one years old before I went abroad. Although middle-aged, I did not even know what a ferry looked like. But we set off to Ireland to test the water, so to speak, before embarking farther afield. I found that my long-lost family was alive and well in County Mayo. During this profoundly emotional time, I wrote everything down. After showing it to my mother, who had been put in touch with a cousin whom she thought was dead, I put my account away in a drawer, where it lay for ten years. Later this formed the basis of my first book.

Living life to the full, we pushed back the boundaries of our endurance, explored new horizons, and did what we could while we could, so that we would not say "if only". Some years later, our exploits were dramatically cut short as my husband became ill and we faced other challenges, eventually giving up riding. Using part of my name as a pen name, I decided to write about our story. So a new career was born as I climbed a steep learning curve. Initially publishing with an organisation in the U.S., I eventually decided to become an indie publisher. I had skills and wanted control to explore all distribution outlets.

With more words flowing, my genre range expanded as, in retirement, I found a new career. Now I continue to wear many hats and push out my boundaries through writing, marketing, formatting, publishing, blogging, tweeting, maintaining three websites, connecting with like-minded people, and generally making a nuisance of myself.

I wait with baited breath for what life has in store as I explore new horizons into the 'third-age'.

ROSALIE MARSH is an award-winning author, speaker, learning & development consultant, grandmother, blogger, marketer, educator, website editor, and indie publisher. Born in Lancashire and settling in North Wales with her husband and growing family, Marsh followed a varied career in banking, sales management, and adult education before "retiring" to concentrate on writing, drawing on her skills and experiences in travel, and adult education. The Just Us Two travel-writing series is based on biographical travel experiences. The Lifelong Learning: Personal Effectiveness Guides aim to inspire you to push out your boundaries and achieve your goals in life. Website: www.discover-rosalie.com

Rachael Rifkin

AGE OF EXPLORATION

WHEN I WAS GROWING UP, summer vacations meant hiking in Mammoth Lakes, California. After the first couple of consecutive years, I was ready to go somewhere else. We used to go other places — Palm Springs, Big Bear, San Francisco, Arizona, Utah. We even went all the way to Disney World when I was seven. So I began looking through the American Automobile Association book for some new ideas. Maybe my parents had forgotten what else was out there.

They hadn't. I'd point out a place and my dad would say, "What are we going to do there?"

"We could do anything! What do we do in Mammoth that's so fun? We hike."

"Exactly. Let's go back to Mammoth."

And so it went until I graduated from high school. I had been accepted into a couple of Southern California schools, so my parents and I went to visit them. Every campus I visited left me with a funny feeling. I was always eager to leave.

I had also been accepted into UC Santa Cruz. My parents did not offer to take a trip up there. That made my decision easier: Santa Cruz it was.

"But it's so far away, and you haven't even visited the campus," my parents said. My grandmother sent me a newspaper clipping of an article that talked about the increasing dropout rate among UCSC students due to feelings of isolation. I balked.

If I had visited UC Santa Cruz before I went, I probably wouldn't have liked it. But it had one thing going for it that the other schools didn't — it was over 400 miles away from where I grew up. I was ready to be somewhere else.

Santa Cruz was beautiful. The campus was in the middle of a forest, with the occasional deer family wandering about. I loved navigating my way around the campus and city. I walked and took the bus everywhere. I explored.

I didn't really like UC Santa Cruz, though. Turns out, I did feel isolated. There wasn't a lot to do, and I was surrounded by people who went out of their way to appear unique. Instead, it was just a different kind of sameness. By my sophomore year, I was contemplating escape again. This time I wanted to go somewhere I liked. I wasn't going to just escape for the sake of escaping anymore.

It didn't take long for me to figure out where I wanted to go. I had always wanted to go to the Netherlands. I had grown up reading Anne Frank's diary and knew that she adored her adopted country. The first thing she hoped to do after the war was to become a Dutch citizen.

I wanted to go to the Netherlands to see what she saw in the Dutch and walk through the same space that she had shared with her fellow Secret Annex housemates. I just never thought I would go. My parents certainly weren't going to take me. When I was younger, it never occurred to me that I might eventually be able to go on my own.

I decided to look into studying abroad in the Netherlands. I discovered study-abroad programs at three colleges, one of which was an international school. I started the process, but it didn't feel real. I couldn't believe I might actually go somewhere I really wanted to go.

I collected recommendations and transcripts, wrote essays, and mapped out how taking this semester abroad would affect my ability to graduate on time. Every time I handed something in, that little, excited feeling would build in my chest.

My parents worried about my safety, but they weren't going to stop me from going. They knew my aversion to paperwork, so I think they were hoping I'd forget something and not be able to go. But by the end of the school year I was all set. I was going to study abroad in the Netherlands from August 31, 2001, through December 15, 2001.

To me, the Netherlands represented exploration, freedom, and the fulfillment of a long-held desire. I'd be on my own in a way I never had been before. It meant I had to trust myself to navigate a new country. Even better, it gave me the opportunity to get to know myself anew, without the weight of parents, friends, or American culture on my back.

For the first time, I felt in control of my life, and it inspired me to do other things I wanted to do. As soon as I got home for the summer, I rearranged my room so it had a better flow. I asked my friend to teach me the guitar. I got an internship at a local paper. A high school friend introduced me to the guy who would become my husband.

Over in Holland, I continued to take risks, and the more I took, the easier they became. When I had moments of self-doubt, instead of giving in to them, I'd take a deep breath and remind myself that taking a chance was always worth a try.

I enjoyed my classes and how open and direct Dutch people were. I learned how other cultures view the U.S. I traveled and made friends that I still have today. I got to know my husband over the phone and fell in love with him. And I finally visited Anne Frank's house, saw where she hid and what she saw in the Dutch people.

In short, I found a place of my own. Now when I travel, my journey is about discovery, not escape.

RACHAEL RIFKIN was inspired to become a ghostwriter/ personal historian by her grandfather, who wrote a memoir about his time serving as a medic in the Korean War. Her blog, Family Resemblance (www.lifestoriestoday.com/blog), features selections of her grandfather's memoir and stories about the traits we inherit, whether genetically or environmentally, and the qualities we find only in ourselves.

Mary Hamer

BREAKING OUT OF THE LIBRARY

THIS IS A STORY OF ESCAPE — though a slow release from sucking mud rather than a daredevil exit down castle walls on a rope. How I released my imagination, that's the story.

It began the day I was returning from a sabbatical to the college where I'd been teaching for ten years. As I looked 'round the familiar setting, the sun-filled lobby lined with mailboxes, the green upholstered chairs grouped in the common room, one powerful thought — or was it intuition? — transfixed me: *I shouldn't be here.*

It was alarming. I'd given my life to education. Scholarship girl, Oxford, Ph.D. That meant a certain limited kind of writing. Correcting papers, marginal notes, final comments to help my students. And during vacations — only then — writing and research of my own. Ever since the day when I was given a shiny green fountain pen for my sixth birthday, in a secret, unknowing kind of way I'd set out to be a writer.

But where had writing as a professor gotten me? How muffled and anxious my voice was. I can see that now. My first book, *Writing by Numbers: Trollope's Serial Fiction*, was about the way the Victorian novelist, Anthony Trollope, worked. He kept count of the number of pages he wrote every day, anxious not to be lazy, not to be in the wrong, anxious to please his editors with the correct word length.

Only after my book was published did I begin to wonder how much of his fears I shared. And why wasn't I writing novels of my own? For three days I sat paralysed at my desk. I wanted to write a story, but I couldn't do it. I gave up and went back — but not entirely to my old ways. I began to question the connection between my own life and the topics I was choosing to research.

That name, 'Trollope'? Was 'trollop' how I'd been taught to name a woman who knew what she wanted? How I'd been taught to think of my deepest self?

What in fact did I want?

All I knew, that day back at work after my sabbatical, was that I didn't want *this*, the college. I went home that night and told my husband I needed to give up my job. He was quite startled. It meant doing without my salary, and we still had kids at home. For myself, I knew I was making a huge decision. I'd clawed my way up to some kind of perch in a very competitive world. I'd be letting go.

But instead of a sickening plunge, what followed was a release: My voice was freed. In fact, my whole body felt free. Those first days I literally rolled on the floor in my study, bubbling with joy. More mature activity followed. But it was no coincidence that I then wrote a book, *Signs of Cleopatra*, about the way Europe learned to condemn a woman with a mind of her own and the power to do what seemed best to her!

My new state of liberation gave me the nerve to choose boldly. I set off on research trips, to Egypt, to Venice, to Rome. I searched out experts in art history, history of costume, Egyptology. In the process of meeting these strangers and being treated with respect by them, my confidence grew.

I began to read the literature I used to teach with new eyes. In a move to re-educate my body as well as my mind, I took actor training: a month's intensive with Shakespeare & Company in Western Massachusetts. That taught me to find the voice that comes from deep inside.

Another book followed. I wrote about Shakespeare, how he used the old stories to get his audience to ask questions about political and religious authorities — those very authorities who had subdued me and blinkered my vision as I grew up.

As I wrote my next book, about children and damage, in order to build my argument, I moved from the voice of the teacher into the voice of the storyteller. Perhaps, deep down, I'd been a secret storyteller all along, but it had been knocked out of me at school. My old kindergarten teacher had to remind me of the day I kept our class of five-year-olds spellbound, telling them the old fairy story of the Hobyahs. I'd forgotten that such power had once been mine.

What now? I asked myself one day in 2003. And then I remembered Rudyard Kipling, the man I'd wanted to study for my Ph.D., though my supervisor had vetoed that idea. Free now to explore him, I read my way into Kipling's life. I began to realise I'd been treading in his footsteps — India, the East Coast of the U.S., South Africa, his home in Sussex — preparing. I seemed to be on some sort of track, ready to reconnect with myself.

Deciding to follow the course of his life was one thing: Choosing to write about it in the form of fiction, rather than biography, was a massive leap. I'd never written anything but criticism before. But confidence and stamina had built up in me, and I was no longer looking for permission or waiting for someone else's timetable.

And so I came to write my novel. In the end, it was not just about Rudyard Kipling. His story led me to that of his sister, Trix, also a writer, but a woman who lost faith in her own voice. Turning my back on life in college that fateful day opened a path that led home, back to what I knew for myself! It worked. *Kipling & Trix* won the Virginia Prize for Fiction.

MARY HAMER was born in Birmingham, England. Educated at the Catholic grammar school and at Lady Margaret Hall, she grew up a secret rebel. Reading Kipling's *Jungle Book* in the small branch library in Harborne offered her the first hint that there was a different, more exciting way to see the world. Mary is married, with grownup children and seven grandchildren. *Kipling and Trix* is her fifth book and first novel. Please check out Mary's website: www.Mary-Hamer.com

Angela Marie Carter

POETRY SAVED MY LIFE

We don't have to die in order to stop living. In fact, most of my childhood and teen years were a form of sleeprunning (not to be confused with sleepwalking), which led to my one and only suicide attempt.

At around 15 years of age, I made a decision to play Russian roulette with medication. I lay there accepting my fate, genuinely spoke to God for the first time, and felt a longing for the future I had just robbed myself of. I survived, and it was the first near-death experience of my many near-life experiences.

It took me many years to learn how to live. I used to think I was cursed. As a child I was molested and lived in a household of alcoholism, neglect, and abuse. When I did tell someone, silence followed. Not long after, I was sent to live with my grandmother and, even to her dying day, she was never aware of my secrets, although she was aware of how broken I was.

I believe that, even from a very young age, poetry saved my life. It was a constant companion that appeared instantaneously after I was abused. I had never been introduced to writing, and more than once was told it was a waste of time. Poetry was a friend I would ignore for several months, but it would always return when I needed it most — something I had never encountered with any human being.

My constant fears put me in dangerous situations that I now look back on and cringe at. As a teenager I found myself in physically and sexually abusive relationships, and constantly in debt with my past. It was important to me that I not be neglected, even if it meant that I nearly died in the process of getting attention. I can remember covering handprint marks around my neck and convincing myself that pain was all I deserved. Depression controlled me, while the person I wanted to be lurked in my shadow and was disappearing.

I thought if I escaped my hometown in Virginia, I'd escape the cycles I'd fallen into. At 18 years of age, I received a scholarship to study at the University of Bath, England. I was a girl from a town of 280 people, studying in a foreign country! When I fell in love with the idea of being unknown, and the possibility of rediscovering myself, I stayed. I met the love of my life, married, and was blessed with the gift of a child. But not even 3,736 miles could save me from the curse. You see, the curse was not out there; it was inside of me. After freeing myself from familiar territory, the past revisited me in new forms that were equally, if not even more, destructive than those of my past. Bulimia controlled my every move for over five years.

I returned to Virginia with my husband, and we welcomed a second child. It was then that the depression almost fully consumed me. I was a living zombie, but my love for my chosen family outweighed it, so much so that I made the decision to admit myself into a program for treatment of depression. I waved goodbye to my daughters in the backseat of my husband's car, and I wore a hood over my head until I entered the building. As I went up the elevator, I thought of how most mothers were creating their children's lunches from organic foods, while my family was driving me to the front door of a hospital.

Throughout all of the bad, one constant friend was always there: poetry. Although I had muted my external voice, I found a new one through writing. I have never been a book-smart kind of person, but I believed with every piece of my being that I was gifted the ability to write poetry so that I could help others. Whereas I once felt that I'd never be any more than a victim, I began to see good in it. A new world formed, one where I was more aware of how universal secrets truly are. I learned through sharing my writing that it is not what happens to us that truly damages us; it's how we — and others that we love — choose not to acknowledge it.

Since that time, I have used all my energy to help others. I have had many defining moments in the last few years, but one marked my most gutsy moment ever. I recently spoke, in public, about what it is like to be a child who is abused. I owe this power and strength to poetry. Not only do I have a voice, I use it to speak of all the subjects that many will not talk about.

Sometimes we have to save ourselves. I saved myself by breaking silence, and reaching out to others through poetry and public speaking. I offer therapeutic writing coaching, coordinate a local poetry group, and have a forthcoming poetry book being published. I accept any opportunity, no matter how small the crowd, to let others know that silence is not golden.

My husband calls me brave — because it was my choice to save my own life and gain the confidence to share what was always there — a beautiful woman who is not cursed, but instead has chosen to help others. In fact, believe it or not, I wouldn't change a thing about my life. Sometimes our gutsy moves save many lives, even if we believe we have only saved our own. Sometimes seeking help is the bravest thing we can do.

Not dying may seem elementary; but living is, after all, a choice. Sometimes it takes us awhile to end up where we need to be. Taking my time didn't make me any less gutsy. It just makes my remaining days very precious.

I intend on making every instant be about helping others find *their* gutsy moment.

ANGELA MARIE CARTER, author of the forthcoming poetry memoir *Memory Chose a Woman's Body*, grew up in a small Virginia farming town. After moving abroad for several years as an adult, she returned to sweet Virginia with her new family and newfound voice, to speak of her trials. Angela offers her poetry and public speaking as a voice that proves silence is not golden. www.angelacarterpoetry.com

Kathleen Gamble

Finding My Way Across Continents

I WAS BORN IN BURMA and grew up on five continents. When I was 18, I went to college in the U.S., my passport country. It was very difficult for me. I was used to adjusting to new places and blending in, but this time was different. I looked and talked like an American, but I had no knowledge of popular culture or how to identify with my fellow classmates.

My roommate had never been out of her home state except to go to college. She spent her time telling wild high school stories. I thought since she was telling her stories, I could tell mine. That was a mistake. *"I learned to drink beer at the Hofbrouhous in Munich. I skied at St Moritz. I walked around the Parthenon and Knossos."* Of course she could not process my stories and said I was a liar. She told everybody I was a liar. I was ostracized, and if I tried to speak to any members of the "group," I was ignored. I thought there was something wrong with me. I could not understand why they were so strange and closed-minded.

I was very naive about the U.S. I had been in multicultural environments my entire life. I knew there were bigoted people, but I didn't understand how it manifested in society at large. One day I went to lunch in the cafeteria, saw a long empty table, and thought, "I'll sit there, and then maybe I'll meet some new people." Well, as lunch progressed people sat around me, but they were all black and none of them would speak to me. The next day I commented on it and was told that whites were not "allowed" to sit at that table. It was for black girls only. I thought that person was kidding. But she wasn't. It was too bad, because those young black women surely had a very different experience from mine, and I probably could have learned some things from them about their perspective of America.

Halfway through my freshman year an old friend from high school showed up for a visit. As soon as I saw him, I knew everything was going to be all right. He knew exactly what I was talking about and assured me I was not a crazy, stupid idiot. Eventually, I made other friends, and things turned out OK. However, I stopped telling my story. To this day, I don't volunteer anything about myself unless I know the other person's story first. Then I usually adapt mine to his or hers in a way that person can relate to.

Twenty years later I ended up in Moscow, Russia. My husband was a Russian-American who grew up speaking Russian at home and had relatives in Moscow and St. Petersburg. He moved there in the 1990s and decided to open his own business. I moved to Moscow not knowing much about it and not knowing the language at all. I landed there with no support system. I was on my own. My husband was working most of the time or out with his Russian buddies.

I was horribly unhappy at first, but what I ended up doing — and what saved me — was two things. I cooked, and I wrote. I made everything from scratch. I often could not find what I was looking for, so I improvised. I pored over cookbooks. My husband was always dragging people home for dinner — mostly Russians who were happy to eat anything I fed them. I think I fed half of Moscow. I was fearless; everybody was a potential guinea pig. And then, by a weird twist of fate, I became the editor of the American Women's Organization newsletter.

In the end it all came together, and I edited, designed, and produced the AWO Moscow cookbook. By that time I was an old hand, and everybody knew me. I was satisfied, and I was content. I had carved out my new persona.

All those years growing up in places like Mexico and Nigeria taught me to have inner strength and to be creative. We never had all the things we needed or wanted, but we found ways to get around that. If Christmas trees were not available, we made one out of paper or cards or cloth. We always made each other's birthday cards. We rarely had TV so we read, played cards, or listened to music. When we lived in Lagos I went to boarding school, so I didn't have any friends to hang out with. But there were always new things to see, experience, and learn from all around me. I never felt lonely or bored.

We became such a tight family unit that it didn't really matter. I think that is why I had such a hard time in the beginning in Moscow and in college. I didn't have the support system people need in those situations. Whether it is an old friend, a family member, or a new friend who "gets" you, as long as there is somebody telling you, "No, you haven't lost your mind," it really helps. But when there was no support system, I was able to find something I really loved to do and enjoyed the ride. An open and curious mind always helps.

KATHLEEN GAMBLE was born and raised overseas and has traveled extensively. She started journaling at a young age, and her memoir, *Expat Alien*, came out of those early journals. *Expat Alien* was published in 2012, and Kathleen recently published a cookbook, *52 Food Fridays*. Both books are available on Amazon.com. You can also follow her blog at www.ExpatAlien.com.

Benny Wasserman

A Teenager Who Cared

*"The glory of friendship is not the outstretched hand,
not the kindly smile, nor the joy of companionship;
it is the spiritual inspiration that comes to one when
you discover that someone else believes in you"*
—Ralph Waldo Emerson

For many years I told people a book by Jack London turned my life around. It turns out the teenager who gave me that book was more important than the book itself. In the end, it was this high school friend's faith in me that changed the course of my life.

My father was fifty-two when I was born. He was a poor, Polish immigrant who could hardly speak English. When I was seven years old my mother committed suicide. My father physically and verbally abused me most of my childhood years. Whatever respect I had for him was based on fear.

From the time I was eight years old I had some kind of a job. Everything from sweeping floors and handling paper routes to working in a bakery and driving delivery trucks. By the time I was twenty, I was working in a slaughterhouse killing cows.

Although I'm ashamed to admit it, I was also involved in criminal activities that could have resulted in prison sentences. Fortunately, my life turned around before I got caught. I don't paint this picture of my youth for sympathy. I do so to show what a high school friend was dealing with when he tried to have some positive influence on me. He was dealing with a functional illiterate who had no self-esteem or self-worth.

Now for the part of this story that has meant so much to me for the past forty-six years.

What is important about this story is not how much time I spent with my high school friend, but the incredible compassion and faith he had in me. I had no idea at that time that another teenager would become so concerned about my future. I now believe that what he did for me during the following eight-year period was just part of his benevolent and charitable nature.

It all began in my friend's backyard when I was sixteen years old. We had just finished playing stickball. I was about to get on my bike to go home when he told me to wait a minute. He ran into his house, came back out, and handed me a book to take home to read. All he said was, "See if you like it." I said nothing.

Nobody had ever loaned me a book to read. I took it home, kept it for a couple of weeks, and then returned it — unread. He never asked me if I liked it or not. If he had, I would have made something up. There was no way I was going to read a book.

During the following two years he loaned me three more books. It never occurred to me to wonder why he was loaning me these books, and I never asked. I never read any of them.

Before my friend went off to college, he asked me which college I was going to. When I told him I wasn't going, he asked me why not.

I told him because my father couldn't afford the $75 for tuition. He then asked, "Is that it?" I said, "Yes." Of course, I lied. I had no intention of going to college. I hated school with a passion.

The following day my friend knocked on my door at home and handed me a check for $75 signed by his father. He said, "I think that should do it." I could only shake my head in disbelief. What could I say, except thank you?

Two years later, while on a college break, my friend came to visit me. He asked, "How's school?" My face turned red as a beet. I had quit college three months after I enrolled. I told him that it just didn't work out.

By then I was working in a slaughterhouse. It was 1954, and I was twenty years old. My friend suggested I join the Army for a couple of years to sort things out. So that's what I did. Unfortunately, I came out of the Army with no more vision of what I wanted to do with my life than before I went in.

As a result of the training I had in the Army, and the GI Bill, I was able to attend an *unaccredited* trade school for radio and television repair.

At the age of twenty-four I got married. Although my friend was unable to attend the wedding, he sent us a strange wedding gift: A book! Inscribed inside this book were the words: **"To the Wassermans on Their Wedding Day."** That was it!

With the encouragement of my wife, it took me two years to read the book. Each time I learned the meaning of a new word, and there were 747 of them, my self-esteem and self-worth took a giant leap forward. My life was never to be the same again.

Slowly but surely I became addicted to reading. My newfound fascination with learning would never end. This experience was not only responsible for me becoming an aerospace engineer for thirty-five years, but more importantly, it led me to other books, which were responsible for allowing me to raise my children so differently from the way I was raised. I was able to break the cycle of violence. And all of my children have advanced degrees.

Oh yes, the book was **Martin Eden** by Jack London. And that high school teenage friend, who never lost his faith in me, was **Carl Levin, who is presently serving his sixth term as a U.S. Senator from my home state of Michigan.**

BENNY WASSERMAN was born and raised in Detroit, Mich. A graduate of Central High in 1952, he served in the U.S. Army 1954–56. He attended a trade school to learn radio and TV repair from 1954–1956. Benny got his associate of arts degree from Pierce College and majored in sociology at UCLA. Benny married in 1958 and has three sons (one physician and two attorneys) and nine grandchildren.

Benny was an aerospace technician, engineer, and manager from 1958–1992. He retired at age 58 and became an Albert Einstein impersonator, which he continues doing today. His book, *Presidents Were Teenagers Too,* was published in 2007.

Alana Woods

TREKKING ACROSS THE UK

I N APRIL 2013 I was in the United Kingdom helping my oldest
daughter cope with three children under seven: two boys, six and two,
and a new baby girl. After the birth I stayed on because daughter and
her man were getting married on 1 August in Italy and daughter had
asked me to stay handy.

End of June saw my husband, John, touching down at Gatwick
and, after a week of the boys and him getting reacquainted, we took
off to do a few weeks' travelling. No point getting under the son-in-
law's feet.

We spent a week touring Ireland, visiting John's ancestral roots,
and then headed back to the UK to undertake a walk we hadn't long
known about. The famous Alfred Wainwright's Coast to Coast Walk.
John had seen it on TV in Australia before flying over. You cross the
UK from the Irish Sea to the North Sea, starting at a little village called
St Bees and finishing at Robin Hood's Bay.

The 200-plus-mile walk takes you through the Lake District, over the Pennines and across the Yorkshire Moors just a little way down from the Scottish border.

We knew it wasn't going to be a walk in the park. We'd booked through a company called Mac's Adventures, and the company website lists it as four out of five in difficulty. But we figured, *We're Aussies; we can do it.*

And we were right; we made it, no disasters. But, and it's a big but, it was a real test of stamina. And that's taking into account the best weather the country had seen for years. That meant no armpit-deep bogs to sink into — only ankle deep — no soaking wet clothes to peel ourselves out of every evening, and no howling gales to pitch ourselves against.

And thank goodness for that, because just walking those distances — up to 16 miles a day — up and down mountains was shattering enough.

Tradition is that you take a pebble from the beach at St Bees and dip your boots into the Irish Sea. Then at the end you drop the pebble and dip your boots in the North Sea.

Second day in we were in the Lake District and, despite what I've said above, the weather was horrible. The guidebook advised against tackling peaks in bad weather, so we took the low route. But at Loft Beck there's no escaping a stiff climb from one valley to another — in icy, sheeting rain, with gusting, howling winds. About halfway up I had to give myself a stern talking to. I was darned if I was going to be the one they had to send in the rescue helicopter for that day.

> The second day in and the weather is foul,
> we're scaling Loft Beck and the wind it does howl,
> what I would give
> to be sure I will live,
> is everything I'm carrying to survive.

> The rain stings with little bullets of ice
> that hit my exposed bits like pellets of rice,

it cascades down the rocks
soaking my socks,
I have doubts I will ever revive.

The wind roars and blows,
I can't stem the flow from my nose,
snot flies to every point in the land
because I daren't spare a hand.
All I want is to safely arrive.

We had two truly shattering days in the walk. The first was the last day in the Lake District, the 16-mile Patterdale to Shap leg, with no teahouses, pubs, shops, or anything else to ease the pain. My God! There's the last peak, Kidsty Pike, then there's traversing Haweswater Reservoir, which the guidebook describes as "Soon you're panting like a hippo on a treadmill." At the end of that, you leave Lake District National Park and start picking up a few C2C signs. By then, if I'd had the breath to say it, I would have been calling, "My kingdom for a teahouse!" We were total ruins by the time we reached that night's accommodation, *much* too tired to eat.

The Pennines and moors provided great, expansive views and lots of boggy ground to skirt. An unexpected sight were the Nine Standards, ancient sentinels against no one knows whom or what. I imagine one day they'll be cordoned off like Stonehenge, but for now we cheerfully sat on them while taking a lunch break.

By the time we arrived at Ravenseat Farm, several hours on from the Standards, we were gasping for the tea and scones the farmer's wife, Amanda, is famous for. We weren't sure she'd be open because she'd given birth to her eighth baby less than a week before. But she was! Serving everyone herself. Now there's a gutsy story for you! I loved the 'Warning. Free range children' sign at the gate.

The Yorkshire Moors were a delight. Comparatively easy up-and-down-dale walking with long stretches of rolling tweed colours. We were a couple of weeks early for the moors in all their purple heather glory, and I was sad about that. It would have been a memory to keep forever.

For all its fame, the Coast to Coast isn't an official walk, so there are no signposts in the national parks, and they make up quite a percentage of the distance. In the Lake District, successive walkers have built stone cairns to indicate the path, but it's not foolproof. We wandered off onto nonexistent paths numerous times, sometimes following other walkers who were going somewhere entirely different!

The last day was the second of our shattering walks. The North Sea came into view miles before we hit the coast, and the first town of any size we spied was Whitby, with its abbey ruins standing proud and alone on the cliff. But there was still a hell of a way to go. By the time we saw Robin Hood's Bay, we were almost too tired to make the steep descent to the sea, where we found the tide out and had to walk halfway to France to reach it!

Would we do it again? Not on your Nellie! Got nothing to prove by repeating it.

But it has given us a taste for more walking. I think that's pretty gutsy of us.

ALANA WOODS … intrigue queen. As a novelist, that's me. I toyed with 'thriller queen' as an author description, but my novels are much more suspense intrigue. I'm a storyteller from way back but not a prolific producer. It can take me years to be satisfied with the quality of a story and how I tell it. I have two suspense intrigue thrillers, a short-story collection, and a writing guide published to date, and I'm reworking a third thriller that should be out this year. Quality is the name of the game, and it's what I strive for. Website: http://www.alanawoods.com

Ginger Simpson

THERE'S NO GENIE IN THE BOTTLE

I MARRIED MY HIGH SCHOOL SWEETHEART and expected us to spend eternity together. He worked as a police sergeant, and I spent my days as an academic counselor. Like most couples, I thought we had a perfect marriage — the average American family: two kids, two cars, two careers. I couldn't have asked for anything more. One of our sons was grown and married, and the other had just graduated high school. And then after thirty-two years, the proverbial crap hit the fan. I'm not sure how or, more importantly, *why*, but my husband found something he loved more than me: Jack Daniels.

At first the occasional drink didn't concern me, but when his JD over ice became a nighttime ritual, I decided it was time for a talk. I told him I didn't understand how a non-drinker suddenly became someone who imbibed regularly. I tried to make him see how insecure his drinking made me feel. I offered to go for counseling, but he insisted everything was fine. Of course, I continually asked him if I was the reason he turned to alcohol, but his answer was always "no" — he was completely happy and only drank to take the edge off his day. He promised to stop, but what he actually meant was he wouldn't leave the booze where I could find it. Yet, every cabinet I opened had a bottle inside (some filled, some half empty). Even the peg boards in the garage had JD hidden behind them; still he insisted he didn't have a problem.

Even when forced by his supervisor to go for rehab, he lied and told me he'd volunteered to go for *us*, but I later discovered the program wasn't his choice. He either went or was forced into retirement. So, yet another lie to placate me.

Wanting someone to change isn't enough. That person has to *want* the change, and he obviously didn't. I don't think he believed I was strong enough to honor my threats to leave. His ten-day rehab proved a waste of time that didn't kill his desire to drink but made him a tearful drunk. He obviously got in touch with his emotions but only exposed them when he drank to excess.

At a time when I was looking forward to midlife security and being proud of our achievements as a couple, I had to decide if living in continued fear of what I'd find when I walked inside the front door was worth it. I'd already found him passed out, with a cigarette smoldering on the carpet and the house in disarray, more times than I could count. Our youngest son had long ago stopped asking his friends over because his dad didn't grasp the concept that we all shared the same home. Our feelings ceased to matter.

The day I came home and found my husband — this man I had loved for so many years — passed out, naked, and soaked in urine, his usual cigarette burning yet another hole in the carpet we couldn't afford to replace, was the day I decided to make the change. I couldn't stand one more minute questioning my own integrity. Had I caused him to turn to drink? I went to an Al-Anon meeting and listened to stories like mine, but no one there had solutions. Others continued to live in the same hell, day after day, but I knew I couldn't. My choices were pretty limited. If someone refuses to change, your only option is to remove yourself from the situation. I'd moved right from my parents' house to a duplex I shared with my new husband, so I'd never lived alone. Could I find the inner strength I needed?

Starting over at forty-nine wasn't an easy decision to make. Somehow, I mustered my determination, packed some clothes, and walked out, leaving him with the house I once loved and everything except the few things I needed. Luckily, I had shared my story with a co-worker, who gave me a key to her house and told me she had an extra room. I took her up on the offer. Living in one bedroom surrounded by nothing that belonged to me was hell. I don't know which was worse — my living arrangements or my continuing efforts to work things out in my head.

I'd tried to make my husband understand that love is composed of trust and respect, and every time he lied or I saw him in a repulsive state, the loss of trust and respect chipped away at that emotion. I'd often wondered about the saying "I love him but I'm not 'in love' with him" because it didn't make sense to me. Suddenly, I knew what those words meant.

God granted me sisters for moral support and one, thankfully, for financial. With her help, I was able to get into my own apartment for the first time in my life and see what being independent was truly like.

Once our house sold, my husband relocated to the apartments next door to mine. I tried several times to tell him I was moving on without him, but apparently he didn't believe me — or didn't want to. In desperation, I put my feelings in writing and explained that I couldn't help him heal. In my written plea, I also told him I wished him well, would always care for him, but in order to open new doors, I had to close the old ones. That was my determining moment — picturing him standing on the other side while I moved blindly into a new life, not knowing what to expect. That decision was the most frightful I've ever made. Sometimes, the unions we think are the best are missing elements we don't realize until we seize the moment and make a change. It was the most difficult, gusty move I've ever made, but it worked out for the best.

GINGER SIMPSON decided to attempt writing her own novel in 2002, and in 2003 her first offering, *Prairie Peace*, was published. Since then, she's dabbled in other genres but always seems to migrate back to her favorite historical era. As all authors continue to learn through the process, so has Ginger, and her debut novel has been recently released with a new cover and title, *Destiny's Bride*. Although her biggest dream has been saying "yes" when someone asked if her book was available at Walmart, she's been happy with the progress of her e-books. After repeated questions, however, she recently tucked one of her books into her coat and smuggled it into Walmart just so she could take a photo of it on the store's best-seller shelf. She never said it had to stay for long. http://www.gingersimpson.com

Jennifer Barclay

Not My Dream, But My Life

I SPENT MY FORTIETH BIRTHDAY not being whisked away to a Spanish city for a romantic weekend, as had been hinted in what now seemed the distant past, but weeping and shaky with my parents. This wasn't how it was supposed to be.

My life had seemed to be coming together, at last settling into year two with a nice man. We were talking about moving somewhere beautiful together. Then he changed his mind.

For a while, the only option was falling apart at the seams.

All I'd wanted was a simple, comfortable happiness at the centre of everything: helping me to be the person who sang tunelessly as she cycled to work in the morning, had good friends and a fulfilling job, and got out into the countryside on the weekends. I'd lost not only the potential love of my life, but my love of life. I hated being a miserable me who cried herself to sleep on friends' couches.

How did other people manage to stay in stable relationships? What was I doing wrong? Gradually, I started to think of a better question: How could I take action to make myself happier?

I was suffering from more than heartbreak, clearly. It hadn't felt like I was in a rut. But now, when I asked myself what I would really like to do with my life, I realised I'd been putting up with things because I thought they were temporary. I had to replace the plans I'd made with my ex and come up with new ones. The age of forty seemed the right time to take a good, hard look at what I wanted.

Why wait for someone else to change my life? In fact, I was lucky: Now, there was only myself to consider. I'd so often compromised for a partner.

Two years earlier, I'd been invited for a weekend in the country, where I was surrounded by happy couples with beautiful children. I'd felt inadequate for two days, and the dinner on the Sunday evening was offering much of the same. Then one of the father-husbands asked me if I'd been on holiday that summer.

'Not yet,' I said. 'My job's always busy during the summer. But next week I'm off for a week on my own in Ibiza.'

His jaw dropped, and his eyes assumed a dreamy look. 'I would *kill* for a week on my own in Ibiza.'

All those people in their seemingly perfect relationships had others to think about. I only had myself. In fact, I almost had a *duty* to think about myself, and about how to be happy on my own.

Holidays on Greek islands always gave me huge amounts of joy. My love of Greece started when I was a child on family holidays and continued into my university years, when I travelled around with a friend. I'd spent a year there after university, when I'd been feeling a little lost career-wise and didn't know what to do. Then, Greece had been the answer — could it be the answer again? In recent years, holidays on Greek islands for a week or two snatched from my busy working year always left me feeling rejuvenated and wanting more. I wondered about going for longer, perhaps a month: two weeks of holiday and two weeks working remotely from there.

My boss took some convincing, but finally I had a month on a Greek island to look forward to: a month to swim in the sea; walk in empty hills; sit in the brilliant, warm sunshine; a month to think — but not too hard — about who I was and what I wanted to do next with my life. In the meantime, I'd put relationships on hold, and I'd start escaping from the never-ending cycle of work, beginning with a freelance day per week, taking a pay cut to invest in my future.

On my first morning waking up on the island of Tilos, with a view of deep blue sky and mountain from my bedroom window, and the glittering sapphire sea through my bathroom window as I brushed my teeth, I knew I'd done the right thing. In fact, it felt like the cleverest thing I'd ever done. Happiness is easy sometimes, as a Greek friend had once said.

I'd work in the peace of the morning, with sweet smells from the next-door bakery wafting up onto the terrace. At lunchtime I'd plunge into the sea, maybe doze a little in the sun as I dried off. After an afternoon of work, I'd walk around the bay, admiring the light and inhaling the fragrance of herbs on the hillside — herbs I'd pick to sprinkle over a simple dinner. In the evening I'd sit out in the balmy air and look up at the stars.

Halfway through my month there, I was snorkelling in a pretty pink-sand bay with my new friend Dimitris, when he found a fat red starfish and put it in my hand. I felt its feelers on my skin, then let it float gently down to the sea bed. Swimming back to the same spot ten minutes later, I saw it had fallen upside down and was slowly, slowly turning itself the right way up. Perhaps that's what I was doing.

It was hard to leave Tilos at the end of that month. But I'd got my mojo back. And I thought of it not as an ending, but a beginning. Strong again, I decided what to do: not what was sensible or expected, but what felt right for me. The taste of freedom, working from home on a sunny Greek island, showed me the way forward. I could do it.

I used to have recurring dreams of Greek islands, especially in winter when things looked bleak. I'd see myself walking in sunshine on a wild hillside with clear blue water below, then into the whitewashed alleyways of an old village. Now that's not my dream, but my life.

JENNIFER BARCLAY is the author of *Falling in Honey: How a Tiny Greek Island Stole My Heart*, and blogs about Greek island life at www.octopus-in-my-ouzo.blogspot.com. Her first book was *Meeting Mr Kim: Or How I Went to Korea and Learned to Love Kimchi*. She is also the editor of many travel-related memoirs. Having worked as a literary agent and then an editorial director at a publishing company, she now works freelance from her home office as a writer, editor, writing coach, and agent (www.jennifer-barclay.blogspot.com).

Laura Mchale Holland

NEW LIFE

THE ICELANDAIR FLIGHT taxis down the runway. I peer out the window, a brown suede shoulder bag clutched to my chest. Moments later, the jet lifts off and zooms toward the clouds. New York City shrinks, the North American continent recedes, and it hits me: We're crossing the Atlantic; there's no turning back.

I open my bag to affirm the traveler's checks, passport, and open-ended return ticket are tucked where I last saw them — about a minute ago. Also inside is a note with the address of a friend of a friend in Switzerland, along with a list of youth hostels in Europe.

It's 1973. I am twenty-three years old, and I feel like my adult life so far has been a great, big zero. No, scratch that. It's been a negative number. I just left a man 13 years older than I am. A man I met when I was eighteen and confused. A man I never loved but married anyway because I thought I'd never be able to leave him. A man who recently threatened to kill me. That jolted me out the door, at last.

Now I am about to land in Luxembourg without a plan. I might be crazy; I don't know. I've attended night school, and I want to return to college full-time. But when I think of sitting in a classroom with students several years younger than I am, I can't imagine what I would say about myself. That I could have gone to college right out of high school, but put it off, stumbled instead into things that ripped me apart and left me that way? That I allowed myself to be so completely controlled by someone that I often couldn't even speak? That I don't know if I deserve to have any hopes at all? Not exactly good ice-breaker material.

I want to create a new life, a different me. Flying to a continent where I don't know a soul may be foolhardy. But I've heard that young people from all over the world hitchhike and ride trains throughout Europe, and the people there welcome them. I thought I'd give it a try.

I nap during the flight and then delve into *The Teachings of Don Juan* before the plane lands for a stopover in Reykjavik, Iceland. It's 11 a.m. and pitch black when the other passengers and I deplane to explore the wares on sale in the airport store. I admire a brown lopapeysa-style sweater with a yoke of brown, white, and tan. A woman who looks about my age approaches and says, "Nice, huh?" The lenses of her wire-rimmed glasses are slightly fogged.

"Sure is, but it's probably way too expensive for me." I say.

"Me, too. Dan — the guy over there — he's my boyfriend." She points to a tall man with long, wavy red hair. He's wearing a green parka and looking at a jewelry display. "Dan and I have about four hundred dollars to last us our whole trip."

"I've got less than that, but there's only one of me." We both laugh.

"I'm Mags." She extends her hand.

"Laura." I reach out, too, and we shake.

"Where are you headed when we land?" she asks.

"The youth hostel."

"That's where we're going. Let's go together."

"Sounds good to me," I say.

Dan looks up and motions for Mags to come over. "Oh, my guy's up to something. I'll see you later," she says.

After we arrive in Luxembourg, Mags introduces me to Dan and three other young travelers she's just met. We all pick up our backpacks and duffel bags and share a ride to the city, marveling at the breathtaking bridges we pass. Once we're on the street, I find the address of the local youth hostel. Dan studies his map and picks a route. We march off but are soon lost.

"We should ask for directions," Mags says. "Anyone speak French?"

I know a little French, but I'm sure someone in the group is more fluent than I am. After a long pause, I say, "I can try."

I approach a tall woman with black hair and smiling eyes, "*Excusez-moi, s'il vous plaît. Où est l'auberge de jeunesse?*"

She replies with such speed I cannot understand her. I ask her to please speak slowly. She laughs and then drags out, "*Allez tout droit pour un bloc, puis tournez à droite et il sera là.*"

I thank her and tell the group, "We're just a block away."

Mags grabs my hand and says, "You're handy to have around." She pulls me, skipping toward the hostel. I feel a little blush of pride.

In the morning, all those who bunked in the dorms gather over café au lait to talk about where we've been and where we're going next. Mags and Dan are headed for Amsterdam. Two guys from Ohio are meeting friends in Paris. They ask me to join them. I recall staring at posters of Sacré Coeur and Montmartre during French class when I was in junior high. I opt for Paris.

The group of Ohioans and I become siblings for a few days. We buy croquet-monsieur sandwiches from street vendors, tour the Louvre, Musée d'Orsay, and all the landmarks I used to dream about as a child. We talk over French bread, cheese, and wine long into the nights in our *pension*. Then they board a train to Marseilles, and I catch a ride with a Canadian family bound for Madrid. As I settle into a spot in the back of their VW van, a blue-eyed preschooler offers me a bag of trail mix, "Wan' some?" he asks.

"Sure," I say. The van lurches forward. The boy tosses a roasted nut into my mouth. I toss a raisin into his. We continue our game as the van bounces along, and I realize my new life has begun.

LAURA MCHALE HOLLAND is a multifaceted story-teller and indie publisher who has released two books: the flash fiction collection *The Ice Cream Vendor's Song* and the award-winning childhood memoir *Reversible Skirt*. Laura's work has appeared in such publications as *Every Day Fiction*, *Wisdom Has a Voice*, several *Vintage Voices* anthologies, and the original *San Francisco Examiner*. Her prize-winning play *Are You Ready?* was produced by Sixth Street Playhouse and Redwood Writers in May 2014. In all of her work, Laura strives to illuminate truths that are often hidden. Intrigued? Get her newsletter at http://lauramchaleholland.com.

Nancy Sharp

THE GIFT OF BOLD LIVING

THE DATE — JUNE 17, 2006 — was a defining one: widowed and with five-year-old twins in tow, I headed west to Denver. Life in New York City after 18 years just wasn't worth the fast, noisy, people-populating-like-ants, cash-depleting hassles-everywhere grind. Certainly, I was sad to leave behind family and friends, but the prospect of a different life, one that I could invent, was too fierce a pull to ignore. Moving to Colorado was more than the dawn of a new decade (I had just turned 40); it would be my Act II.

Much has changed these past eight years. My twins are 12, I met and married a native Coloradoan, and I became a stepmom to two boys, now 21 and 22. Today I worry about social connections; ample exercise; and too much video time for the tweens; and dating, organization, and career opportunities for the older boys. My new life has broadened my worldview: I can now grill, pull weeds, and even — brace yourself — use a power drill.

By recasting my life, I proved to myself that when the unthinkable happens, we need not be in stasis. Hope and possibility exist, I think, even in the grimmest of times. I should know. My first husband died of a brain tumor at age 39, leaving me with two-and-a-half-year-old twins. Those were hard, hard times. Just when I thought I couldn't see beyond the vortex of grief, I found a shred of hope.

My moment of transformation arrived with little fanfare. While driving with a friend to visit my family in Connecticut, I suddenly blurted out, "Why can't I just move to Denver?" Lisa, my pretty and deeply spiritual friend who knew my longtime love of Colorado, answered, "You can. What's stopping you?"

"Well," I began dismissively, "there's my parents and my mother-in-law. I'd have to buy a house, find new work, find a school for the kids, make new friends, blah, blah, blah."

As the list of why-not-to-move-to-Colorado grew longer, the reasons also became more diffuse. Lisa was unfazed, like a mirror reflecting the longing of my heart. Suddenly, I understood that none of these perceived obstacles came close to what I had already conquered. Just like that, my decision was made. I'm not a runner and never will be, but the surge of energy I felt at that turnkey moment could have propelled me to run the New York City Marathon.

That's the upside of change: the adrenaline-pumping feeling of **hope**. Losing my husband to cancer changed my life forever, but moving to Colorado gave me hope that a new life was possible. What does this really mean? In my view, we can choose not to be defined by the past. We can sweeten our lives any moment, any time. That's right.

You might be thinking, "Well, she had extreme circumstances." Yes. Extreme events can lead to dramatic changes, but sometimes the opposite is true. It's easier and safer to stay put when life mows you down. But is it wiser? Saner? I felt stuck for a full two years before making my move. I put on mascara and dragged myself to work, made Mickey Mouse pancakes for my active toddlers, even dated a little. I tried to be positive about my future, but in reality, I was just getting through the days. I didn't live my dreams. One day bled into the next, and that is how I passed the time. It's human nature to want to be fixed in time. But at what cost?

I had no grand plan when I moved to Colorado beyond the desire to claim breathing space for the twins and me. I knew that I was a skilled enough writer to be able to find consulting work when I was ready, just as I knew that I would branch out beyond my one friend in Denver (my college roommate). Since all expectations of the world I once envisioned for myself had already been crushed, I found a strange calm in starting anew. Everything felt fresh and exciting.

It was in this spirit of bold living that some seven months after arriving in Denver, I reached out to a widowed TV news anchor who was selected as one of the city's "Most Eligible Singles."

What did I have to lose by writing him? Maybe we could be friends?

I had never even heard of Steve Saunders before reading about him in the newspaper, nor did I know about his equally well-known father, a veteran print journalist.

I fired off an e-mail and a photo to Steve letting him know that I was new to Denver and that I was also widowed with two children. I proposed that we meet for coffee.

Two weeks passed. No response.

Maybe he never received the e-mail?

In a burst of courage, I decided to resend it. This time Steve responded within the hour, apologizing for his slow response. He wanted to talk. He wanted to meet.

Dinner lasted four hours. At first we kept the conversation light. (I really was curious to know what it was like to be a TV anchor in Denver.) But ultimately we began to trade "war stories" — the toughest moments for him during his wife's illness, the worst times for me, the gray aftermath of living with loss, and, of course, the way our losses had affected our children.

We had many dates in the months that followed. They were fun, light, and adventurous. And so began the process of blending two families. By then we knew we wanted to marry. The love we had found in one another was real and true. We understood how the past crept into the present, but in each other were able to discover peace and joy in living every day. Our story is still being written, still being lived, past and present and future at once. In the words of Joni Mitchell, *"Well something's lost, but something's gained."*

To bold living!

NANCY SHARP is the author of *Both Sides Now: A True Story of Love, Loss, and Bold Living* (Books & Books Press, February 2104). She frequently speaks to large groups about bold living, contributes to *The Huffington Post*, and writes the blog Vivid Living: Life in Full Bloom…Thorns and All. ™ Website: www.nancysharp.net/

${Robin}$ ${Korth}$

THE DAY I STARTED TELLING
MYSELF THE TRUTH

IT WAS AN AUGUST AFTERNOON IN 2006. I was standing in the quiet of my living room. The "whoosh" of the air-conditioned air coming from the vent above my head made the silence hard to ignore. The room felt very large. I felt very small. My husband had moved out two weeks earlier. My son was away at summer camp. My daughter was somewhere else. I was utterly and totally alone — not a single soul needed me or cared where I was. The chill of this truth arrowed into my heart, and I began to cry. Then I began to sob. Then I howled. The pain and the tears took me to the floor.

I was 51 years old, with not a clue as to how I had gotten to this place of feeling so solitary and undone. Life had treated me badly. I had done everything right, but it had just come out wrong. How could this happen? Who was to blame? I remember eyeing that terribly cold room as if the answers might be found there. As if someone would walk in the door and say, "Gee, Robin, I am at fault. Let me fix it all up. I'll make it OK." But no one was coming. I was the only one there.

Then the bomb exploded. *"It's you,"* said a voice in my head. *"You are in this room, here and now, because you* chose *to be. Isn't it time you took a good look? Perhaps it is time to do something about what's going on in your life."* The challenge of these words stopped my self-pitying tears as I just sat there — very, very still. I then wiped my smeary nose, and I chose. I chose to start telling myself the truth.

My marriage was in serious trouble because I had grown lazy, selfish, and scared. I had stopped talking to my spouse or showing my real self to him. Our relationship had slid into a black hole of us each "doing our own thing" and meeting at meals to talk over the future of our children or the price of a new computer. I could not remember the last time we had shared anything intimate or heartfelt. It had been too easy to go to sleep each night denying that anything was wrong. The intimacy of sharing the same bathroom and bed now masqueraded as a full and loving partnership. I had done nothing to stop the march of this sad show.

My eyes widened as more truth seemed to just rise up from the floor. Where was my daughter right now? I assumed she was safe, but I knew nothing of the specifics or people who filled her spirit and her days. She had gone away to school, and I had let her slip from my grasp. She came home on weekends here and there. We smiled and we shopped. We watched a movie or two. I asked how she was and she told me fine. My daughter was an "I love you" stranger now. I had let this happen.

My son was at camp in upstate New York. His almost-teenage-hood was messy. He wasn't happy or doing as well as he could. I had so easily marked all the stuff off on his "must-have" summer experience list and just given him over to someone else's care. What was really going on with my boy? Did he cry at night? Was there a young woman who longed as much for his smile as he did for hers? Besides loving math and computers and white-sauce pasta, what was special to him? I didn't know these answers. I had been too wrapped in my own lostness, in my own I-don't-want-to-look fear.

I did not know my husband, my daughter, my son. I did not know myself. I had set us all aside and apart from myself. This truth — that I was responsible for my being alone and terrified — caused sweat to prickle my armpits and my breath to come short. My choices and actions had brought me to this place of soul-shattering despair. I remember looking slowly around that room where I sat, seeing it all so differently now as this truth sank home. In that single moment, my life went from outside to inside. Inside, where I understood, finally, that *I create it all*.

How powerful I was! Look at what I had done. What could I not do if I chose differently and acted differently? My heartbeat was a peaceful cadence in my chest as I sat on that floor, clear-eyed and calm. I was done. No more denial. No more blaming others. No more hiding from the painful stuff, being lazy and soul shy. I was going to start living my life with conscious choice and honest good care.

My life of deep personal truth began on that hot August day. But it did not end there, not by a long shot. The journey of self-honesty is a day-by-day, get-braver-as-I-go sort of thing. It means being kind and patient with myself, too. For so much of what I hold as "true" are things I never even thought to question before. In the setting aside of old habits and old thinking, I allow the inside of me to come blossoming forth with wonder, curiosity, and love. Living this way brings a power and a joy to life — and an ability to share myself with generosity and openness — that I choose to never, ever let go.

ROBIN KORTH is a renegade and an outlaw. She is also an international speaker, writer, and businesswoman. Number four in a family of seven children, she grew up in the uncluttered scrub palm neighborhoods of Miami, Florida, in the 1960s. After years of doing life as she was "supposed to," Korth walked away and began doing life from deep inside.

She captures her experience in her book *Soul on the Run*, published by Balboa Press in May 2014. *Soul on the Run* is Korth's courageously honest exploration of the power and joy that living is meant to be.

In 2013, Korth launched her information and blogging website, which generated more than 40,000 likes on Facebook in its first year. She also introduced the "Robin in Your Face" daily motivational app, which has been downloaded thousands of times across the globe. She is a divorced mother of two, has a friendly rescue dog named Scruffy and a self-assured cat named Sean. For more information, visit www.RobinKorth.com.

Reading Group Guide

Dear Readers and Book Clubs,

We hope that following questions will stimulate you and members of your reading group to interview one another. Ask someone in your group to share his or her own gutsy story, or pick questions that relate to your favorite authors in the anthology.

1. Out of the 46 stories, which one did you relate to the most and why?
2. Do you have a gutsy story to share?
3. What pushed you over the edge to make this gutsy decision?
4. Was it something in the back of your mind for years, or was it a sudden decision that "I've got to do this"?
5. How did you break this decision to your significant other and your children (if applicable), and how did they take it?
6. Once you made this decision, did you really think it was right or did you still have doubts?
7. What's the difference between being "gutsy" and being selfish?
8. Did you persuade your partner to come along, did he or she come along reluctantly, or was he or she as eager as you right from the start?
9. What would you have done differently in retrospect?

10. What was wrong with your current life that you had to change it?
11. Did the adventure change you?
12. Is this change permanent?
13. Do you need another adventure to stay motivated?
14. Do you need another adventure now?
15. There is an external "gutsy" adventure as well as an internal one. Which one is more difficult? (Example of internal gutsy change: deciding to write a book on *How to do Everything and Be Happy* after the loss of a loved one … Peter Jones, page 1.)
16. Some people have a "gutsy" promise they won't give up. (Example: Susie Mitchell, page 112, who would not let her pregnancy or childbirth get in the way of her training for the World Championship in track cycling.)
17. How did you decide it's more important to do what you love than to make a living?
18. If you're dragging people with you on this "gutsy" journey and they're unhappy, at what point do you say, "My dream is not worth sacrificing my family for?"
19. Is there a compromise: a mini-gutsy adventure?
20. Does being "gutsy" entail danger?

If you'd like to share your thoughts or report your club's discussion, we'd love to hear from you. Thanks for choosing *My Gutsy Story® Anthology: Inspirational Short Stories About Taking Chances and Changing Your Life.*

If you enjoyed the book, please tell your friends. Please send your comments to: Sonia@SoniaMarsh.com

Also by Sonia Marsh

WHAT DO YOU DO when life in sunny Southern California starts to seem plastic, materialistic and just plain hellish?

For Sonia and Duke Marsh, the answer was to sell their worldly goods and move to an unspoiled, simpler life with their three sons in Belize, Central America, a third-world country without all the comforts and distractions of life in the developed world.

Sonia hopes the move will bring her shattered family back together. She feels her sons slipping away from her, and her overworked husband never has time for her or the boys.

This is the story of one family's search for paradise. In this memoir, Sonia chronicles a year of defeats, fears and setbacks — and also the ultimate triumph of seeing once-frayed family ties grow back stronger from shared challenges and misfortunes. For Sonia, paradise turned out not to be a place, but an appreciation of life's simple pleasures — a close-knit family and three well-adjusted sons with a global outlook on life.

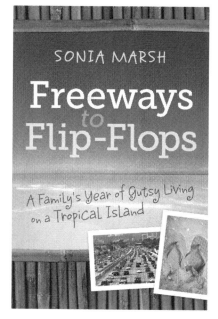

Freeways to Flip-Flops
ISBN: 978-0-9854038-1-1
$14.95

Dear Reader,

I hope you enjoyed the second volume in the anthology series. Please post a **review on Amazon** and/or **Goodreads.** These are always helpful to authors and fellow readers.

If you have not read the first volume in the anthology series, *My Gutsy Story® Anthology: True Stories of Love, Courage and Adventure From Around the World,* it is available on Amazon in print or in a Kindle edition, as well as other e-book readers, and you can request it in bookstores.

My first book is a memoir, *Freeways to Flip-Flops: A Family's Year of Gutsy Living on a Tropical Island.* This is my story about uprooting my entitled teens from Orange County, California, to live in a hut in Belize, Central America. There, we discovered that trading materialism for a simple life on a tropical island helped us reconnect in unexpected ways.

Please e-mail me at Sonia@soniamarsh.com if you have any questions or if you belong to a **book club** and would like me to attend or Skype you during your meeting for a Question and Answer session. You can also connect with me via Twitter: @GutsyLiving, or visit me at Gutsy Living on Facebook.

Thank you for your support.

Sonia Marsh, Author and Editor

Acknowledgments

First of all, I am indebted to the 46 great writers who shared their gutsy stories to make this book possible. I thank them for their willing participation in this labor of love.

Thanks also to Marcie Taylor, who reinforced my idea about starting a "My Gutsy Story®" contest on my blog in 2011. I never realized how many people wanted to share their stories, and I am thrilled to see the audience of writers and readers forming a global community on www.soniamarsh.com.

Eve Gumpel, my fantastic editor, has retained the voices, styles and even the differences between American and British styles of punctuation, and Tracy Gantz is my amazing proofreader.

I am grateful to Michele DeFilippo and Ronda Rawlins of 1106 Design for their professional design and formatting of the anthology. It's a pleasure to work with their team of experts.

I hope you send me your own "My Gutsy Story®." My goal is to create a series that will grow with unique stories from people around the world. I would love to create a global community of gutsy writers. Please follow the series on my website: www.SoniaMarsh.com and let your family and friends know about it. You can also share it on Twitter with hashtag: #MyGutsyStory.

Thank you for participating in this global endeavor. —Sonia Marsh, Editor

About the Author

HAVING LIVED IN MANY COUNTRIES — Denmark, Nigeria, France, England, the U.S. and Belize — Sonia Marsh considers herself a citizen of the world. She prides herself on being a gutsy woman who can pack her carry-on and move to another continent in one day.

As a motivational speaker, Sonia inspires audiences to get out of their comfort zone, take a risk and pursue their dreams. As a book marketing coach for indie authors, she guides her clients to indie success. Sonia welcomes new friends, bloggers, writers and readers at Soniamarsh. com (http://soniamarsh.com). Contact her at: sonia@soniamarsh.com, www.facebook.com/GutsyLiving or Twitter.com @GutsyLiving.

If you're an indie author, she invites you to join her Gutsy Indie Publishers Facebook group. There, you'll find tips from a wide range of writers on publishing and marketing your books.

Sonia's current home base is in Southern California. Stay tuned as she plans her next gutsy adventure with the Peace Corps, where she hopes to serve helping women and children in Africa, the Western Caribbean or Vanuatu in the South Pacific. Stay in touch with her on her blog: SoniaMarsh.com, where you can read about her new adventures and the start of a new life in 2015.

34685507R00117

Printed in Poland
by Amazon Fulfillment
Poland Sp. z o.o., Wrocław